THE LITTLE POTTER'S DAUGHTERS

BERYL ROBINSON

Published by The Robinson House Writers
Arthur Robinson House
13-14 The Green
Billingham TS23 1EU

© Beryl Robinson 2024

Beryl Robinson asserts the moral right to be identified as the author of this work.

All rights reserved. No part of this publication may be reproduced, stored in a retrieval system or transmitted, in any form or by any means, electronic, mechanical, photocopying, recording and/or otherwise without the prior written permission of the publishers.

This is a work of fiction. Names, characters, businesses, places, events and incidents are either the products of the author's imagination or used in a fictitious manner. Any resemblance to actual persons, living or dead, or actual events and places is purely coincidental.

I would like to thank Dorman Museum in Linthorpe, Middlesbrough, for allowing me access to the archives of the Linthorpe Pottery to gain an understanding of the running of the pottery.

The Te Papa Museum in Wellington, New Zealand, for giving me the idea for a novel after seeing their collectors exhibition which included pieces of Linthorpe Pottery.

A big thanks to Gillie Hatton, editor, mentor and friend for helping me to get my books out there.

PROLOGUE

LOTTE AGED 20, WELLINGTON, NEW ZEALAND 2013

Laptop open on the garden table, Charlotte Taylor, known as Lotte, sat, still in her pyjamas, her brown legs on a chair in front of her. Her pretty face was still full of sleep and as blank as the notebook in her hand. She had been sitting like this for some time in the warm early morning sunshine, thinking where to start. She had done the same for weeks, trying to think of something, anything, but no inspiration came. Everything in her life seemed stagnant, taking the path of least resistance. She had even plumped for the journalist/creative writing course of which she was in her final year at college. For her dissertation she needed to write a novel but she couldn't even begin with the first sentence.

She had no life experiences, no life plan mapped out, but drifted by in some chaotic daze. If she wasn't careful, she would remain inert for the rest of her life. Many of her friends had gone to university in Auckland. Others had taken gap years, heading off to all corners of the world, saving indigenous people or endangered animals. She knew all this of course because she watched them doing all sorts of things via social media, always pressing the like button. She rarely wrote anything about what was going on in her life because, the truth was, nothing happened as she remained in the house where she was born.

Her father worked as an industrial cooling engineer. He thought he had made it because he had a company van. As a family they never socialised much except the annual firm's barbecue that her father insisted they all attend. Her mother was a part time shop assistant in one of the small shops in the mall.

Lotte shared a bedroom with her much younger sister, Brogan, so had no privacy to bring anyone home, even if she wanted to. She had hoped to convert the garage into a studio apartment but her gran had now moved in since grandpa passed, leaving her on her own.

She jumped as the patio doors opened and the smell of coffee wafted over to her. As if by magic, gran stepped into the garden with a cafetiere.

"Hi, Gran," Lotte called.

"Oh, hello, lovely. Why are you up so early? Wet the bed?" she laughed.

"No, of course not. I couldn't sleep thinking about what to write for college," Lotte replied.

"What about a cup of coffee to help the brain cells? It always helps me to start the day and you never know I might be able to help," Gran said.

"I'll have the coffee but I need a story and I haven't even started and it needs to be in after the holidays." Lotte moved her notebook to allow her gran to put down the tray.

"Sometimes you don't see what's in front of you when you try too hard. What does it have to be about?" Gran asked, putting down a cup for her.

"It can be anything but it needs to be a good novel really. I just don't know where to start. It all sounded so easy when I started the course." Lotte surprised herself when tears welled up, threatening to roll down her cheeks.

"Why don't you and I sneak off for the morning. Let's go and do something together. We could go to the Te Papa Museum, then we could have lunch in one of the nice little restaurants in the Courtenay Quarter." Gran placed a hand on Lotte's shoulder. "Come on, my treat."

"Okay, thanks. I'll just go and get dressed." Lotte disappeared into the house. It seemed like a better option than anything else she could think of at the moment. She knew she should have made a bigger effort to write. She didn't want to fail her finals but her brain just didn't want to work.

Within fifteen minutes the pair of them had set off, leaving the rest of the house still in their beds. It felt like playing hookey to the two of them. They walked quite quickly through the streets to the Botanic Gardens where they waited for the cable car down into the centre, chatting about nothing much. The view of the city was dramatic. They could see the harbour as they rode the cable car through clouds and down to the business district.

Lotte was surprised how Gran managed to keep the pace going. She was much more active than her daughter, Lotte's mother, who always seemed to lounge about when she got back from work. She was much more fun as well.

The museum had been built in 1998 but still looked modern and it was free. Why didn't she know this, Lotte asked herself as they wandered into the air-conditioned entrance which had a large Maori 'Wharenui' as well as exhibits from 'The Hobbit', one of Lotte's favourite books and films.

The two of them wandered about, Lotte hoping she wouldn't meet anyone she knew from college. It wouldn't be cool to be seen with Gran.

"Look at that, Lotte. There's an exhibition of pottery. It has a picture of a jug on the banner, from Linthorpe Pottery in Middlesbrough, England." Gran walked closer to have a look.

"What's so interesting in that?" Lotte asked, following behind and already feeling bored. The pot was a sludgy brown colour and seemed rather uninteresting yet it had pride of place on the banner.

"Some of your grandpa's relatives worked there. I have two vases from the same pottery at home. Come on, let's have a look to see if I can find anything similar. They were given to us as a wedding present but I never really liked them though didn't have the heart to get rid of them as your grandpa said they were family heirlooms." Gran smiled at the thought. They took a leaflet to find out more about the collection of ceramics.

The rest of the morning they mooched around the market before heading off for lunch as Lotte tried to get her gran to tell her more about her grandpa's family. The harbour area was bustling and they were lucky to get a table outside where they both ordered fish.

The conversation continued when they arrived home, as Lotte followed her gran into her small rooms to look for boxes which had belonged to her grandpa. They had never been opened for years and she wasn't even sure what was in them now, but Lotte was interested in the two vases to see what they looked like.

"I'm sure they were put in the roof space out of the way so you'll have to climb up yourself. There's a light up there but I'm not sure which box they will be in," Gran told her.

Lotte despaired when she saw the number of boxes, considering her gran had downsized. There seemed to be no end of rubbish and boxes lined up along the edge of the roof.

Sitting herself cross legged on the wooden boards, Lotte began sorting through, many of which were fortunately empty. When she finally found the box with the vases, she was underwhelmed as they were the same brown colour and not vibrant or modern. They had the initials KS and CD written on the bottom.

Intrigued, Lotte picked up the box and took it downstairs to look more closely.

She put the vases carefully on the kitchen table then went outside into the garden to sit with her gran while she looked more closely at what was in the bottom of the box.

The paper the letters were written on was fragile, as Lotte attempted to open them, the folds torn. They were well over a hundred years old. The ink had run in places and stained brown where damp had got to them over the years.

"Gran, what do you know about these letters?" Lotte asked. "They are from someone called Kate to a John and Ellen."

"I'm not sure, but if they were in the box with the vases then it's probably grandpa's family," Gran replied.

"The last one mentions a girl called Clara. Have you heard of her?" Lotte continued, looking closely at the date on the letter.

"No, I can't help you there either. Let's have a think… your great grandfather was Charles, his mother was Elodie, his father was a Joseph Taylor. They were still alive when we married. She was a quiet woman."

"Nothing like you then, Gran!" Lotte laughed.

"Cheeky madam." Gran wafted her arm, causing some of the letters to fall to the floor.

"Careful, Gran, these are delicate. Oh look, Elodie is mentioned here. John and Ellen must be her parents," Lotte said as she read more. "They lived on a sheep farm." She was fascinated with the writing even though it was every day happenings.

"The family came from a place called Middlesbrough in

the north of England. That's the connection to the pottery we saw today and the vases," Gran told her.

"Thanks Gran, you have just given me an idea for a story but I'll need to do some research first," Lotte said, folding the letters carefully before putting them back in the box. "See you later."

PART I

CHAPTER 1

KATE STAINBANK AGED 14, STAFFORDSHIRE 1879

Kate Stainbank knew better than to go into the house through the front door. It was only used by the rent collector and the vicar, both had a rap to waken the dead, never mind those hiding inside. Instead, she took herself to the back of the row of houses and into the ginnell which as always was a hive of activity. Neighbours always gathered in the yard to chat, to hang out washing, children playing or sitting in prams and today was no exception. The difference was they were stood in groups, listening to her father shouting behind the closed yard door.

One of the women called to her, "Don't know what your Frank's done this time, lass, but he's getting a right belting from your dad."

Kate didn't answer but her heart was in her mouth. It was strange that her father was home from work so early so something terrible must have happened.

Lifting the latch, she opened the door slowly, shocked to see her brother slouched in a bloody bedraggled heap against the wall. Her father stood over him, belt in hand, still in his work trousers, braces down by his side. His vest was wet with sweat and it looked as though he had been about to get a wash when Frank had turned up.

She had never seen their father take a belt to her brother. The back of his hand, yes, but never the belt. Stepping between them, Kate yelled, "Dad, stop, stop it. You'll kill him."

"Get out of my way, girl! I'll deal with you later. Now get in the house, go on." His voice lowered as he got to the end. "I've been too soft on him, should have took the belt to him afore now but you? What possessed you? Oh, get out of my sight before I do something I regret." The vein at the side of his temple throbbed. He was having difficulty controlling his anger.

Kate stood rooted to the spot as she looked at her brother who was trying to wipe the blood from his face. She was still between them as she said to him, "Go, lock yourself in the lav, go on now."

As her father's anger seemed to abate, she touched his hand. He pushed away, dropping the belt as he walked into the house. Kate followed and he rounded on her. He had never raised a hand to anyone other than Frank but she thought he might do so now. Her mother was sitting on the sofa with Alice on her knee, Rachel beside her, but it was her younger brother, John, sitting with his feet upon the chair, hands over his ears, which upset her most.

Frank Stainbank Snr turned on Kate, grabbing her wrist. "Right, girl, out with it. Have you been helping that feckless brother of yours sell stuff on the black market? Don't lie to me 'cause you've been seen."

Kate burst into tears, involuntarily rubbing her pained and bruised wrist. "I've done nothing, dad, honestly I haven't," she sobbed. "You can ask me friends, they were there."

Her mother, Peggy, was about to speak but Mr Stainbank

put his hand out to stop her, her mouth opening and closing like a fish gasping for air.

Everyone looked at Kate. She didn't want Frank to get into more trouble but she wasn't going to take the blame for something she hadn't done. "Last week a man was waiting outside the school asking me to pass a message to our Frank. I told him to leave me alone but he just laughed and said he would be watching me."

"Why didn't you say something?" Her father spoke loudly but his anger seemed to have gone. He looked tired.

"Well, I gave Frank the message and thought they would leave me alone but yesterday some of them stopped me when I was with me friends." Kate sobbed again as tears fell from her brown eyes.

"Go on. What did they want?"

"There were three men. They stood in front of us, blocking our way. One of them shooed my friends away, and another took my schoolbooks while the third, the one in the middle, grabbed my wrist. I told him he was hurting me but he just tightened his grip. He said they were friends of Frank and they needed me to answer some questions so I had to go with them."

Kate was trying to remember everything. One man had clutched her elbow while the others walked either side. She'd asked where they were taking her and why she couldn't just answer any questions there in the street. She hadn't wanted her father to have another go at her for forgetting something. The man had said, "Because I'm not the one asking so just be quiet and keep walking," and she'd had no option but to be led. There was no way she could have outrun them through the streets.

"They took me to a house similar to ours and I tried to pull back from the step but I was pushed from behind…" She hesitated. She'd almost fallen through the open door and into the hallway. Sitting on a sofa in the living room had been the largest man she'd ever seen. He'd seemed to pour over the sides of the sagging seat. His legs looked tiny in comparison to his fat belly which took up most of the space. His hand moved and someone had pushed her forward. He'd said, "Ah, Miss Stainbank, I hope the boys weren't rough with you." His chins had wobbled as he'd spoken.

She'd tried to tell him that she didn't know what he wanted with her and that she couldn't help, but he'd said, "You need to tell your brother I must to speak to him urgently. It's a matter of great importance to me."

"I asked him who he was," she told her parents, but she didn't have the courage to say that the man had said that Frank knew who he was and she just had to pass on the message.

"I didn't know what to do or say next," she said. "The silence frightened me. I looked for the boy who had my school book. He was close to the door so I moved toward him. They sniggered at me and said they'd be watching me." Her voice was shaking. "I grabbed my books and pushed my way past, running out of the door and up the street as fast as I could. That's the truth, dad, honestly. I've done nothing wrong but I'm scared."

"If that's the truth, our Kate, then that's it. Leave it to me." Mr Stainbank pushed John off the chair and sat down while her mother got up to plate the evening meal.

"What's Frank done this time, dad?" Kate asked as the family were eating the evening meal without Frank. The fight seemed to have gone out of her father, his shoulders sagged. He looked tired, weary even, and Kate felt a rush of love for this man who worked so hard.

"Oh, your brother's only gone and got himself sacked for stealing, the stupid bugger. He's been trouble since the day he was born, that one. He's not right in the head, I tell yer," he replied, shaking his head. "I got him that job at the pottery on my reputation and this is how he repays me. I've got to go and see the Mr Roth, the manager, tomorrow to see whether he is going to involve the police."

No one spoke. What could they say that wouldn't make matters worse.

Frank remained incarcerated in the lav until the family had finished their evening meal. No one spoke about him until Mr Stainbank stepped out for a quick drink. Kate ran out to her brother who was now quivering with cold and shock. There was only eighteen months between them but he was stocky in build like their father. He was struggling to stand as she helped him inside.

"Look at the state of you, boy. I don't know what gets into you!" his mother wept. "Let's get you cleaned up and to bed before your dad gets home."

Frank winced and groaned as Kate watched their mother put a wet rag over his face. He tried to talk but his voice was hoarse, his lips swollen and it looked as though his nose was broken. There were weal marks on his wrists where he had tried to defend himself but he had that arrogance about him as he pushed his mother away. "Leave it," he said gruffly.

No one wanted to speak, to make matters worse. Kate could see her younger sisters were already frightened, huddling together. John jumped when Peggy Stainbank told him to get his brother up the stairs and into bed. Kate decided that was best for them all and took the youngsters upstairs as well.

Mr Stainbank stood in his good shirt while his wife fastened his only tie. He was wearing his ill fitting suit. The sleeves were too long and it seemed he had shrunk since he last wore it. His wife parcelled his work clothes in brown paper which he tucked under his arm, just in case, she had said.

"Good luck, dad," they all said as he headed for the door, all staring at him.

"I'll have to get on my knees and beg the boss not to press charges. I'll kill that lad if I get my hands on him," he said, pulling at his shirt collar as though it was choking him.

"Don't get all worked up. Just listen to what Mr Roth has to say. He knows you're a good worker. Go on now and get it over with," his wife told him, patting his arm.

Kate had her fingers crossed as she watched her father straighten his back before leaving by the yard door.

It was quiet when Kate got back from school later that afternoon. She hadn't been able to concentrate. Peggy Stainbank hadn't heard anything from her husband so it must be good news. He must be at work. They hoped he was at work. If he was drinking, he would have spent all the money they had and life would be far worse. Frank was sitting feeling sorry for himself. He looked terrible but Kate had no sympathy for him. His eyes were turning black, his cheek bone may have been fractured and there was still blood under his fingernails where he had tried to defend himself. Kate didn't want to make eye contact with him. As far as she was concerned, they might live in the same house but she wanted nothing to do with him.

Eventually Mr Stainbank turned up in his working clothes. They were relieved but sat quietly waiting for him to speak. He slowly took his suit out of the brown paper, shaking out the trousers before putting them on the hanger that still sat over the kitchen door. He did the same with his jacket and then turned to the eager faces waiting for the news.

"Mr Roth has agreed not to involve the police this time," Mr Stainbank spoke quietly.

"Oh. thank God, and I'm sorry, that's blasphemy but I'm so relieved that I am," his wife said.

"Oh, I haven't finished yet so don't get your knickers in a twist. Thanks to him," he pointed at Frank who tried to shrink into the chair, "we have been told – not asked, mind you – but told that we will be moving to a place called Middlesbrough to work in a pottery there. That's the choice, police or move," he sighed as everyone seemed to have a question for him.

"Where's that?" they asked.

"I haven't the faintest idea. Up north, that's all I know and we need to start packing to go up in the next week or two."

"What about me school certificate?" Kate cried. "I need to get my certificate if I am going to train as a teacher."

"Thank your brother for that, lass. He's spoilt it for everyone."

The talk around the table that evening was animated with everyone asking questions. Where would they live when they moved to Middlesbrough. How would they get there? On and on it went, with many questions unable to be answered, until they were told to be quiet.

Kate was in a quandary. If she moved before she got her school certificate, her dream would be over. "Why do we have to go now?" she asked. "What about my school certificate?"

"We'll do what Mr Roth tells us to do and be done with it," her father replied. "I don't want to take the family away from all we know but this is the only way to keep him…" He spat the word 'him'. "…out of trouble. What's done is done, now I want to hear no more about it."

Frank still didn't speak even though everyone looked at him. He knew he had messed up this time but his mother would stick up for him. It would be a new start away from his so called friends who got him into all kinds of trouble. He would have to be more careful next time.

When they had retired to bed, Kate lay listening to her parents talking, quietly getting out of bed to listen.

"If it had just been our Frank, I would have let him call the police. It might have done the boy some good. But it was Kate, see. Mr Roth said she would be implicated even though I explained and I couldn't throw her life away," Mr Stainbank said. "She was seen with those men by Mr Roth himself. If the police pick them up, they will implicate Frank and Kate. It would be a wake up call for Frank. But her…? No, I can't let that happen. It would ruin the girl's life before it has begun."

"No, no, oh what a to do," her mother responded. "So it is what it is and we'll have to get on with it."

"I had to take the move, don't you see? If I'd taken a job anywhere else, and I've had offers believe me, then Mr Roth would have had no choice but to call the police and I couldn't throw Kate to the mercy of the courts, could I?"

Kate was mortified. They all blamed her brother but it was her fault. She returned to her cold bed, looking up to the ceiling until she fell into a fitful sleep.

CHAPTER 2

MIDDLESBROUGH 1879

The house was in an uproar as items were packed in crates before being removed again to use and then be re-packed. Peggy Stainbank was a nervous wreck, worrying about travelling so far, to a place no one had heard of. Mr Roth had arranged train tickets for the family as well as the removal of their belongings which looked like a bonfire when piled onto the cart. They left the house in the dark, the only home Kate could remember, the keys left on the back window sill ready for a new family. There was no need to lock the yard gate. Who would want to break in to an empty house?

The family left for Middlesbrough under a cloud but dressed in their Sunday clothes as they set off for the station. Frank was carrying Alice, reluctantly on both counts. His youngest sister wanted to walk but they didn't want to miss the train. He was surly because he didn't want to go, rowing with his mother, telling her he was sixteen and old enough to fend for himself. It was only when she threatened to go to the police herself that he relented. Kate carried a basket filled with enough food for the journey. Only John and Rachel seemed impervious to the impending upheaval.

Standing on the platform waiting to board the train, Kate could taste the soot which was leaving a fine dust on her skin. She involuntarily shivered in an attempt to shake it off. Even though she was only fourteen, she felt grown up sometimes, others still a child. Her excitement and fear were in equal measure.

No one, even Mr and Mrs Stainbank had ever been on a train, all in awe of the big belching beast building up steam on the track. The family took up most of the carriage which was fortunately empty. Kate looked at each one in turn to see what they were feeling about the journey. Her mother was nervous, looking around, continually sorting out the basket to try and keep her hands busy. Frank, he had no expression on his face, as usual. His eyes were as black as night, as though no light penetrated the depths. She worried for her brother and what would become of him if he didn't control his anger. John on the other hand was a quiet boy but his eyes sparkled as he watched the smoke from the train make the people on the platform disappear and then reappear as if by magic. Kate felt sorry for him in a way, the lad was often overlooked for attention. Her younger sisters, Rachel and Alice, climbed on and off the seats in excitement, not really aware of what was going on… to them it was an adventure.

The whistle sounded, the train started to move along the station platform, the guard waved his flag. No going back now. Her own life was on the cusp of something new and Kate hoped and prayed that she would be successful and happy, always happy.

THE FAMILY HAD SPENT the day travelling and it was dark when they reached Middlesbrough Station. Mr Stainbank helped them all down the step and onto the platform. He had arranged a cab to take them to their new home, talking to them all about the new opportunity the family had and how kind Mr Roth was.

The horse clip clopped up a long road until it reached a row of terraced houses, pulling up outside one of the middle ones. Kate thought it was tiny, like a child's house, with a door straight out onto the street and one long thin window. Above were two smaller windows. They would never fit in this house. It was far too small, much smaller than the one they had left behind.

Mr Stainbank jumped off the cab, paying the driver before helping them all down, their legs stiff from sitting for so long. Taking the keys out of his pocket, he opened the front door, ushering them all inside. It looked very cluttered with their boxes. Kate looked around. They had walked straight into a living room from the street. There was a fireplace on one wall though the grate was empty, lamps alight making shadows. The only other door she could see was at the opposite end of the room which her father proceeded to open saying, "Look, a kitchen with room for a table." The kitchen was just a sink with a cold water tap, an oven and a narrow cupboard. That was all and that was why there was room for a table. Peggy Stainbank looked around her, saying nothing.

The stairs to the upper floor were in the corner, narrow, curving round into the darkness. She presumed the other door led into a yard and the lav, which Mr Stainbank confirmed.

"Wait until you see upstairs," he said, lifting one of the lamps. "Follow me."

There was only room to go up in single file as they slowly followed him up the stairs, bumping into each other on the small landing where there were two doors and a wooden ladder leading to the roof space. The first had just enough room for a double bed but the second larger room had a double and a single bed which was to be the girls' room. The lads were under the eaves. Frank said nothing but she could see John was pleased. He wouldn't be so close to his brother, though she felt sorry for him, and relieved she wouldn't have to go up and down the ladder on a regular basis.

A welcome cup of tea was made while sharing out what was left of the food in the basket, before looking in the trunk for the girls' nightclothes. The two youngest climbed into the double bed, clinging to each other for warmth but they would both soon be asleep, leaving the others sitting around a kitchen table.

Mr Stainbank told his family briefly about his work but no one was really listening so he gave his older son a lamp with strict instructions it was to be put out before they fell asleep.

Another was given to Kate who followed her brothers up the stairs. She was dog tired but wasn't sure she would sleep. Her bed would have no warmth from her sisters, and the smells and sounds were unfamiliar, but surprisingly the journey had made her weary.

KATE HEARD her father leave the house the following morning but the rest of the family did not stir, so she turned over and slept until daylight came through the thin curtains at the bedroom window. She got to the staircase at the same time as her mother and they quietly followed each other down the creaky stairs and into the tiny kitchen.

"What do you think, mam?" Kate said in little more than a whisper so as not to disturb the others.

"It's what it is, lass, and we'll make it a home. Your dad's got a job and hopefully Frank will find one soon and we'll be set," she replied, filling the kettle with water from the tap.

Once they were all up, dressed and had eaten a frugal breakfast, Kate offered to take the girls for a walk to see what they could find. John asked to come along and she was happy for him to join them. Frank sat in the chair by the fire, which was out, knowing that this would be his father's seat. She knew he wanted to cause an argument. He loomed threateningly toward his mother who chose to ignore him. What was wrong with him, Kate thought, but certainly didn't say it. She didn't want to be on the end of his wrath. Perhaps her dad was right and there was something not right with her brother's head.

The house stood in the middle of a terrace of twelve houses, regimented like soldiers on parade. Kate wasn't sure which way to go but decided on the opposite way to the way they had arrived in the cab last night.

There were further rows of houses. She saw a building and as they got closer to it, she realised it was a dairy. She wished she had thought to bring money to buy milk. They continued as the road turned. On the left was a dip to a small beck where water seemed to flow unobstructed by the reeds and shrubs along its banks. Ahead, Kate saw a number of large trees so she headed in that direction, taking a struggling Alice firmly by the hand. Realising it was a cemetery, they followed the wall until they reached the iron gates which stated Linthorpe Cemetery. Kate had thought they were in Middlesbrough but this place was called Linthorpe.

"Can we go and have a look at the names on the graves?" Rachel asked rather morbidly.

"Not now, Rachel, maybe later or tomorrow when we have more time," Kate replied. "Look, let's walk to that big building at the end of the road to see what it is."

On their left they stopped to look at a lovely quaint white cottage which was somewhat overshadowed by a much larger building. The sign on the gate said Rose Cottage and it had a small garden with a path down the centre. The door was set back in an open porch with two steps down to the path. On the ground floor, either side of the door were two large bay windows. Kate thought it looked really pretty and she would love to live in a house just like it one day. The building they were heading for was at the right hand side of a cross roads, sitting on the corner. It was quite an imposing building with plenty of windows looking out into the street. Some were open and she could hear voices. It sounded like a school though she couldn't be sure. There was no name on the main door, which was large, wooden and foreboding.

"Come on, let's go back and tell the others what we've seen!" Kate put her arm round John's shoulders. "Are you alright?" she asked.

"Suppose so, no one ever asks me 'bout nowt." He shrugged his shoulders to remove her arm.

"Well, no one asked me either, but let's look at it as an adventure," she said, trying to cheer him up.

"We know whose fault it is. One day I'm going to have to kill him," he said without any trepidation in his voice.

"Oh, John don't say that! He made a mistake but he'll be right, just you see." Kate didn't believe her words but had to say something to her brother, nor could she admit that this time it wasn't really all Frank's fault.

When they got back to the house, Frank was still sitting in the chair as their mother was busy unpacking boxes, carrying items up and down the stairs. Kate opened the door to the yard for the girls to play so she helped with the sorting out while telling her what they had seen. She explained that she had seen no shops but there was a dairy.

Taking money from her purse, Peggy Stainbank turned to her son. "Here, Frank, go and see if you can buy some milk. Ask if they have any work, you might get set on and you wouldn't have far to go," she said with some desperation in her voice, though it would be a brave man to take him on in that state.

Although he grumbled, taking his time to get up, he took the money from her, putting on his coat and shoes and headed out of the door. The mood lightened as soon as he left the room. It was a though a rainbow had appeared after a thunderstorm to Kate.

"I'll go in the other direction later, John. How about it?" Kate looked at her brother who nodded. "I'll take the basket and see if I can get some shopping if you tell me what we want." She wanted to keep her brothers apart otherwise this was going to be a long school holiday unless John found some friends to play with and Frank could get a job which would keep him out of the house. She didn't know whether she should mention what John had said but then decided she didn't want to get him into trouble and he surely didn't mean it.

When Frank returned with a container of milk, he seemed in a better frame of mind. Kate listened while he spoke to anyone who was listening that there was no work at the dairy but in the village was a public house called the Cleveland Hotel where people went if they were looking for work and where they were picked up. He would need some money in case he had to pay someone to put him forward.

"You'd best speak to your father," was all Peggy Stainbank said to him before turning back to her chores.

CHAPTER 3

The family soon settled into their new lives apart from Kate who seemed lost. The neighbours welcomed them, giving them information on where to shop, market days and the vicinity of the local school. Their accents were strange to her and she hadn't seen anyone around her age who she could talk to, though they were probably working somewhere.

She was pleased for John who had met a few boys around his age from the other houses so spent most of his days at the beck where the water trickled slowly. The weather had been dry for a few weeks so he was in his element with boots and socks off, paddling in the stream, playing games in the ginnell or running between the houses.

Frank had surprisingly left the house mid morning with money in his pocket. Kate went over the stilted conversation between her brother and father the night before. It was clear that there was to be no more trouble brought to their door. He was also expected to tip up money every week. Frank had gone to the village and found some work though was vague as to what exactly it was and who for. All he would say was that he was running messages for a local gentleman who expected him to be available at all sorts of hours. It didn't sound like a proper job but no one dared to question him.

Kate spent much of her time helping her sisters with their letters and numbers ready for the new school term. She could stand the confines of the house no longer so wrapped a shawl around her shoulders and headed for the door with her sisters in tow. Walking along Roman Road and into the village, she not only found the weekly market and public houses but also Albert Park. Rachel and Alice were happy to run around with a freedom they lacked in the yard.

They all, except for Frank, took a stroll to the park the following Sunday afternoon which they really enjoyed. They walked past the cemetery, along Roman Road to New Cemetery Road toward the church before entering the gates of Albert Park. The main pathways met in the middle where a water fountain stood majestically. The fountain plaque said it had recently been built to mark the crossroads of the park.

It was as the family were watching the water flow over the ornate bowl that they came across Mr Roth and his wife. They stopped to speak mainly to Mr Stainbank, who removing his cap, folded it uncomfortably in his hands as they were introduced. Kate wasn't sure what to do. She could feel her face redden when her father introduced her. Mr Roth knew of her unfortunate involvement with her brother's old friends, using it as a lever to move the family to the Linthorpe Pottery. Kate was embarrassed that he knew so kept her eyes firmly rooted on the ground.

She was surprised when Mr Roth spoke directly to her, asking if she had now left school, and if she had found any employment since moving. "No, no, I haven't," she stuttered. "I was hoping to train as a teacher."

He asked if she would be interested in working at the pottery as he may have a vacancy. Why didn't she call in the following day and have a chat before she made a decision. Her parents were looking at her expectantly so she confirmed that she would and they went on their way. Peggy Stainbank became excited, talking incessantly to her husband about the opportunity until he told her to pipe down.

THE POTTERY WAS MUCH SMALLER than Kate had imagined, a shed which was bustling with people. Mr Roth welcomed her like an old friend, offering to show her round himself. He explained that the pottery was built to produce original art wares and hopefully would provide work for one hundred men and women. The land had a large deposit of red brick clay which was used to make the pottery. There was an art manager who was responsible for the design and modelling of the pottery. There were trays and trays of pots waiting to either be decorated or fired in the kiln. Mr Roth was keen to tell her that Linthorpe Pottery was the first in Britain to have gas fired kilns where the temperature was more controllable than the log fired kilns.

Kate smiled as his enthusiasm was infectious. He picked up a finished pot, telling her that the gas kiln was the secret to the Linthorpe glaze. It was also very economic because the kiln heated up much more quickly. A Mr Christopher Dresser was heavily involved in the designs, many from his travels to Japan. Kate had never heard of this Mr Dresser but vowed to find out, especially about his travels.

She was taken to a room full of tables where women wearing smocks sat with paintbrushes in their hands. Mr Roth informed her that this was known as the Ladies Finishing Room where designs were put on pots before they went into the kiln to be fired. The colours were set in rough bowls in the middle of the tables on a tray which rotated so the ladies could spin it round to reach the colour they required. The ladies moved to a bench under the window to mix a particular shade of blue or green or whatever took their fancy before returning to their seat. There were rows of jars with what looked like hundreds of brushes in all shapes and sizes sitting in opaque liquid waiting to be used. Mr Roth introduced her to the woman in charge, Emma Waller who said she was from Manchester, though Kate didn't know where that was exactly. Her accent was different to those from Middlesbrough which she also struggled to understand. They seemed to talk very quickly.

Kate and Mr Roth returned to his office where he offered her a seat. She was nervous about the conversation, placing one hand into the other to stop them shaking.

"Do you wish to discuss the opportunity with your parents?" he said. "It would mean putting your plans to train as a teacher on hold."

She agreed, thanking him profusely, saying that she would indeed let him know.

Kate walked to the village, because she wasn't ready to go home, in a daze so she almost missed Frank slipping into the side of the Cleveland Hotel. She stood on the opposite side of the road for several minutes but he didn't reappear. The only movement was a cab leaving from the archway where the drays would enter to deliver the barrels of ale. She couldn't see if Frank was inside but decided it was best if she let him get on with it, whatever 'it' was.

She wanted to get her decision set in her mind before she spoke to her parents so walked slowly home. It would mean giving up the dream of becoming a teacher but she knew deep down that was all it was, a dream. People like her didn't become professional people and she would have to give it up anyway if she ever married. By the time she was in the kitchen having a cup of tea with her mother, her decision was made, she would start work for Linthorpe Pottery the following Monday.

Kate had hundreds, no thousands, of questions to ask her father about the pottery and they started almost as soon as he came in the door. Although he tried to explain that she wouldn't need to know most of it, she was insistent.

Asking him about Mr Dresser, he replied, "He's a gentleman of class with some fancy ideas. He went travelling to Japan and brought back all those silk pictures you see on the walls. We don't see much of him but his art's everywhere."

Kate was intrigued as to what this man could be like. They had only travelled a few hundred miles to Middlesbrough and to her it was the other side of the world. But he had gone all the way to Japan, what an adventure that must have been.

THE FIRST DAY of work was filled with trepidation for Kate. She had barely slept. Standing in her day dress, in the kitchen, she was ready for work long before her father. They walked the short distance to the pottery together, he telling her not to worry, her with butterflies in her stomach. She was so nervous, she felt sick and her legs were shaking. School and teacher Miss Preston belonged in another life. Her father walked her to the door of the Ladies Finishing Room where she looked pensively at the women around the wooden tables which had a mixture of pottery waiting to be worked on.

The silks belonging to Mr Dresser covered one wall. Kate counted thirty-five frames, square and oblong of all sizes. The silks were bold and bright, muted and soft, which seemed a contradiction in terms but they were, she thought, the most beautiful things she had seen in her life. A tall wooden bookcase stood by the wall behind her seat. The dark wood seemed to be covered in a layer of dust. As the pottery was removed, the dust floated into the air, getting into her throat.

The women, Kate realised, knew so much about their job but she was determined to do her best and try to fit in. The older ladies talked amongst themselves so she was pleased to be seated between Rose who was eighteen and Dotty who was twenty-three. They seemed to be able to chatter and work at the same time, their fingers deftly painting the pottery. A stern look from the older ladies soon quietened them down if they were getting a little raucous.

Each of the women specialised in different aspects of the work. Two of them were experts in under glaze decoration where they painted the pottery with coloured paint after the initial firing in the glost kiln but before being glazed. Dotty was an artist decorator using transfer decoration. Rose was the closest in age to Kate and was still training in illustrations, drawing beautiful plants and flowers.

Kate thought she would pick up the work quickly. She was given 'seconds' to work with, pots that had either cracked when they were fired or those which had an air bubble or didn't quite make quality control. All she had to do was practise painting them without paint dripping everywhere. How hard could that be? It proved much more difficult. Firstly she had to learn the technique of not putting too much paint on her brush or it dripped, too little and it left streaks. Kate found trying to turn the pots without getting fingerprints on them also proved problematic. Some days she felt she hadn't progressed at all, going home having achieved nothing.

She found she had plenty to talk to about in the evenings as the family sat around the kitchen table. Everyone listened to the conversation, surprised at the diversity of the pottery and how much there was to be learnt.

She was excited when she received her first wage, two shilling and sixpence, a fortune to her. She gave her mother one shilling and sixpence for her keep. The remaining money Kate decided she would save as much as she could. Well, she didn't have much time to spend it. From her first pay, she gave John, Rachel and Alice a penny each, promising them if they worked hard at school she would give them another one next week.

As time went on, Kate felt very grown up and more confident sitting with her newfound friends, Rose and Dotty. She would listen in wonder at the outings they had. Dotty was walking out with a young man, who by what she told them seemed to be a saint. The thoughts of going out on these jaunts excited Kate but she knew her father wouldn't even consider it until she was sixteen.

Winter turned into spring, then summer as the days became warmer though she always found there was a chill wind in this part of the world. Flowers were pushing their way through the frigid soil so she decided to walk to the park one Sunday afternoon to try and find some inspiration. John agreed to escort her – they had become closer as they grew older – and Rachel and Alice joined them, running ahead.

Kate looked at the colourful array of nodding flowers dotted around the flowerbeds. The colours ranged from sunflower yellow to cornflower blue to rose red. It gave her inspiration and the fresh air cleared her head. The assortment of leaves from the trees were in all shapes and shades of green and she picked up several to try to copy at work.

She hadn't been very good at drawing at school but was determined to try her best though she thought her flowers all looked the same. Over the weeks and months her work didn't seem to improve dramatically and she was beginning to worry Mr Roth would think he had made a mistake in taking her on.

CHAPTER 4

It was early 1881 and only a few weeks before her sixteenth birthday when Kate heard two pieces of news. One excited her, the other filled her with rage and dismay.

Dotty had talked incessantly about a concert which was to be held at Albert Park Hotel which had a large room where her beau would be singing in the choir. She was able to get tickets for anyone who wanted to join her. Kate really wanted to go so was determined to ask her father. She had enough money of her own to purchase a ticket but was worried about his reaction.

Amongst the rest of the conversation which seemed to drift from one subject to another somewhat randomly, Dotty mentioned the drawings for her portfolio were ready for her examination.

Kate's head turned quickly, asking Dotty to repeat what she had just said. What examinations? She wanted to know and why hadn't she been told about them? The room went quiet, all looking directly at her as she jumped from her chair as though she was on fire.

"I'm going to speak to Mr Roth," she said and before

anyone could stop her, she was out of the door. Her bravado left her as soon as she walked out of the room but she continued through the factory where no one took any notice of her, weaving between the benches.

Mr Roth's office was in a separate building so Kate continued across the courtyard, knocking on the door before she could think of the consequences. There was no reply which she was thankful for but she knocked again. As she was turning away, she heard a noise which sounded like someone saying "enter" so she pushed the door open.

"Oh, I was hoping to speak to Mr Roth," Kate said, looking at Mr Woodman, who she wasn't fond of. He was a brusque man, red cheeked with very bushy sideburns. She wasn't sure what else she could say, wanting to close the door behind her but thought she had come this far so she stood her ground. "I've just been told that some of the women are studying for examinations and I'd like to try," she said without drawing breath.

"That's impossible. Now get out, I'm busy," Mr Woodman replied gruffly. His face seemed to be getting redder by the minute.

"I've got my school certificate and I'll work hard." Kate gained in confidence, thinking he didn't look very busy.

"I'll hear no more of it. Now get out of my sight."

"I'll wait and speak to Mr Roth then," she retorted but rushed out of the door when Mr Woodman picked something up from his desk.

"Get out," he yelled as she slammed the door just in time to hear something crash against it. What a horrible man, so different to Mr Roth. She would wait until he returned from wherever he was but she wasn't going to let the matter drop.

"How did you get on?" Dotty asked.

"Mr Roth wasn't there and Mr Woodman seemed to be in

a bad mood so I left it," was all Kate said as she got back to her work. She didn't want to go into any details of the one sided conversation.

It was later in the day as they were packing up to go home that Lydia Palmer, one of the older women, asked her for a word. Kate always thought Miss Palmer was old fashioned, a spinster, though in truth she didn't know much about her. She really belonged in neither camp. Dotty, Rose and Kate were looked on as the young ones while the others hung on every word of their supervisor Miss Waller, leaving Miss Palmer on her own. With that realisation, Kate immediately felt sorry for the woman.

"I'm not sure how to say this, Kate, so I'll just come to the point. Did Mr Woodman proposition you?" Lydia Palmer asked.

"No, of course not. Whatever made you think that?" Kate asked, looking incredulously at her colleague.

"He has done it before so just be careful that's all I'll say. Just be careful," Lydia continued as they walked out of the room together.

As she walked home, Kate went over the brief conversations with both Mr Woodman and Lydia Palmer but could really make no sense of either. In the end she thought she had probably had a lucky escape as far as Mr Woodman was concerned but also thought she should make more of an effort to befriend Lydia Palmer.

The other matter of the ticket to the concert could be more difficult to secure. Her father was very strict and his word was law in the household. Kate waited until they were all sitting round the table, except for Frank, before she started the conversation. She put forward a very good argument as to why she should be allowed to go. After all she was a grown up, sixteen in a week, earning her own money and more to the point, she never asked for anything, ending her monologue with a plea to her father.

At first he said emphatically no, putting all obstacles in her way… it would finish too late, she couldn't walk home alone in the dark, on and on he went but Kate was having none of it. Her brush with Mr Woodman had given her a confidence so she answered him back for the first time in her life. She would ask John to walk to the concert with her, she would come back in a cab with the others, she had enough money to pay for it. To finish off, she told him it was a Saturday so she didn't need to be up for work the following day. Anyway, she had promised her friend Lydia Palmer, who poor soul, never went out and she couldn't let her down.

In the end of the somewhat heated conversation, her father relented, making her a very excited young lady, counting out her money several times so she knew she had enough to purchase her ticket for the concert.

Soon enough, it was Kate's Saturday night jaunt. The damp rags that had been put in her hair gave it a curl. She brushed at it until it shone, finishing it off with a pink ribbon. She had also polished her shoes until she could almost see her face in them. Her Sunday dress she thought dowdy but it was marginally better than her work dress. She had butterflies in her stomach as John made a big thing of it, offering his arm, making her feel a young lady, as the two of them left by the front door.

Her brother waited with her until her friends arrived. She kissed him gently on the cheek before turning to go into the large hall. There were what seemed like hundreds of chairs standing to attention, row upon row and it was a free for all to get the best seats with a good view. The room had a whiff of damp coats, varnish and cheap cologne but that didn't dampen the feverish humour of the audience.

The women from the pottery sat together, talking animatedly. Kate could hardly contain her excitement, looking around the large room as it filled up with people. The front rows were reserved for dignitaries, the mayor, local businessmen and their wives. She spotted Mr Roth, Mr Woodman and their wives, and nudged Lydia, who looked round in her chair to see them arranging themselves in their seats.

Suddenly there was a hush around the room as what seemed like dozens of men proceeded to get into position on the stage. The choir master explained the programme for the evening, finishing by inviting the audience to a cup of tea in the kitchen after the singing.

Kate was enthralled by the harmonies; she could feel the hairs on the back of her neck stand up making her shiver joyously. She couldn't believe how the men, some of them quite large in stature, could make such a heavenly sound. One or two of the songs she knew, hymns, but others she had never heard of in a strange language which she didn't understand but that didn't matter to her.

At the short interval, the audience shuffled in their seats, coughing and whispering, while Dotty was in her element, explaining to the women what would happen when they moved into the kitchen. The room became eerily quiet as the men once more took to the stage, taking their positions while Kate looked at the faces along the rows. She sat with her hands folded, wanting to tap her feet but thought that might be too common. The voices rose to a crescendo before becoming silent as one. The audience clapped their hands enthusiastically between songs before shuffling to a standing position for 'Land of my Fathers' then 'God Save the Queen'. There was a fraction of a second delay as the choir master turned, men bowing, before the whole room exploded in applause and whooping and hollering in appreciation. The noise startled Kate who thought the end would be more restrained but was happy to join in. The second half had been just as beguiling as the first and she knew that this would be the first of many concerts. She just loved it.

Kate and Lydia went to find a large table to seat both the ladies and Dotty's boyfriend while she went with Rose to get the tea and biscuits. Once they were all seated, Dotty craned her neck to look for her young man, Wyn, who walked over with a number of other men from the choir and proceeded to cause an uproar as they moved spare chairs from other tables. They were all introduced. Ted Williams held Kate's hand a little too long, making her blush. As she looked at him, his eyes sparkled. His hair was coal black which curled tightly around his ears, there was a dimple on his left cheek and his smile lit up his whole face, giving him an angelic look though his eyes were full of mischief and Kate was smitten. The rest of the evening went by in a blur as they laughed while the men continually ribbed each other, comfortable in each other's company.

Mr Roth and his wife came over briefly to speak to the ladies, making Kate embarrassed. Feeling in a mischievous mood herself, she asked about Mr Woodman saying, "Is that his wife he's with?" The whole group looked over, catching Mr Woodman's eye which is exactly what she hoped, wanting him to know that she had the ear of Mr Roth so he shouldn't cross her.

All too soon the evening was over and while Dotty's boyfriend and Ted Williams went to get a cab, the ladies headed for the cloakroom for their wraps. Kate was the closest so she was dropped off first, Ted jumping out to help her down the step. Putting her hand to his lips, he brushed it gently. She knew she should take her hand back but she couldn't. She wanted to feel this young man close to her. Propriety got the better of her as she thought her father may be watching so she shouted, "Goodnight," before turning. She heard Ted whisper, "I'd like to see you again, Miss Kate Stainbank," before jumping back into the cab, shutting the door and they were away. She wanted to laugh at his cheek and forthright manner but grinned at the thought of seeing him again.

Quietly removing her outdoor clothes so as not to disturb anyone, she climbed the stairs to her cold bed. Hugging herself she went over the night, not the concert, but Ted Williams. Oh he was so handsome, so wonderful, so funny. There was a cadence in his voice when he spoke which meant you were not sure if he was being serious, until his eyes lit up, his lips creasing at the corners before he burst out laughing. His lips, oh his lips. She could still feel the brush of them on the back of her hand. She didn't know what this feeling was, it surely couldn't be love, but she did know she was smitten with Ted Williams, and as she closed her eyes, she hoped he was equally smitten with her.

Sunday morning she spent telling the family all about the concert, not mentioning Ted Williams, she wanted to keep him for herself for now. Kate could hardly wait for work on Monday to find out what the others had to say.

Dotty didn't mention Ted, she was too busy enthusing about Wyn, and as Kate didn't want to sound too keen, she only joined in the conversation regarding the concert. They all agreed that they had had a wonderful evening. Even Lydia concurred that she would love to join them if they went again.

CHAPTER 5

It was the Thursday of that week when Kate's bubble finally burst and it was nothing to do with Ted Williams but from another source altogether.

She had wandered toward the hot house to see if any items were ready to be brought through to the finishing room. They weren't really running short but she wanted to stretch her legs as well as escape Dotty's infernal chatter. Kate had wanted to shout at her to keep quiet as she was infiltrating her thoughts of Ted which was making it difficult not to speak of him.

The shelved trolley stood outside the hot house full of items to be brought through to the finishing room, so she went to look for the two orphanage boys who moved the trays about. It was as she stood that she felt the warm breath of someone standing very close behind her. Trying to turn, Kate caught her foot on the trolley as Mr Woodman, she just knew it would be him, tried to grab her. Flinging her arm, she caught him on the side of his neck with her broken fingernails, but worse, her arm came down, catching his braces as she fell backwards, he on top of her with a tray of vases smashing all around them.

Suddenly the whole area seemed full of people trying to help them up. Blood was pouring from Mr Woodman's neck while Kate pushed herself up, cutting her hand on the broken pottery now littering the floor.

"You'll pay for this, Miss Stainbank," Mr Woodman shouted. "Come to my office when you've cleared up this mess."

She was shaken not only from what had happened but what he would do. Someone brought a brush and shovel which she snatched from them, sweeping somewhat manically while blood dripped from her hand. Tears pricked her eyes, all thought of Ted and romance gone, that bubble temporarily burst, as now she would have to have her wits about her. Kate didn't want to talk to anyone about what had happened otherwise the tears would fall. So she finished clearing up, marching through the pottery and into the courtyard where she stood for a few minutes, taking great gulps of air. Straightening up, wiping her dusty, bloody hands on her apron, Kate knocked loudly on the office door where she hoped to see Mr Roth.

Unfortunately for Kate it was only Mr Woodman sitting behind his desk, blood now drying on his shirt collar. He didn't ask her to sit but began his tirade against her which she felt was best to try to ignore by not responding. However she wasn't cowed but stood upright, eyes looking directly at him as he continued. He could sack her, he could fine her the cost of the lost pottery, or she could become his mistress to pay the debt so to speak. What was it to be?

To say she was shocked at the latter was an understatement but she continued to glare at him, speechless at his impudence. It was something she would never agree to, never.

Pushing his chair away from his desk, he indicated she should come closer. His whiskery jowled face smirked at her expectantly.

"No, I won't. I want to speak to Mr Roth," Kate said, keeping her distance.

"Ah, your good friend Mr Roth. Well, let me tell you, girl, he's not here. He's in London with Mr Dresser so I'm in charge while he is away. What have you got to say to that?"

Kate continued to stare at him. What could she say?

"Cat got your tongue? Not so bold now, are you? I could countenance your study if you accept," he said.

Kate was afraid he would get up from the chair so she moved to the door saying, "Do what you wish, Mr Woodman, but I won't go quietly. I'm sure your wife would be interested in what you are up to here at the factory. I'm sure Miss Palmer would back me up so think on." With that, she ran out, slamming the door behind her.

The women had heard what had happened and were waiting expectantly for Kate to come back to confirm the story. She flounced in, saying he had threatened to sack her or make her pay for the damages. She explained that it was his fault as he had come up behind her. They all agreed that she would have to be careful as he was a nasty man. The whole mood in the room had been dampened. Kate kept her head down so no one would see her tears.

Mr Woodman remained in his chair, his face a shade of puce, as he thought of that girl. She had picked a fight with the wrong man and he was determined to have her out of this place. He would have to put a plan into action before Mr Roth returned or he would need to be more careful. He was determined to make her his mistress. She had a fire about her which he would love to tame.

As they were leaving for the day, Kate asked Lydia if she could spare a few minutes but she needed to get home as her mother was ill. Kate walked with her, explaining Mr Woodman's 'offer' which she had rejected, obviously, while apologising for dragging Lydia's name into the conversation.

"I'm sure it won't come to anything but can I have your word you would back me up?" Kate pleaded.

Lydia Palmer felt she had been compromised but would stand by her new friend and said so. It cheered Kate up no end to know she had an ally against Mr Woodman but knew she would have to be careful and keep out of his way until Mr Roth returned, hoping he would speak for her.

When she got home, she relayed the story again, leaving out the conversation with Mr Woodman. She knew her father would have attacked him and she couldn't live with his sacking as well as John who was now working squeezing the clay through canvas sheets to reduce the moisture. It was a heavy job rotating the plunger but his physique remained slight. Trying hard to make light of it, she made her father promise not to interfere, as she said, she was sure Mr Woodman would see it as an accident.

"Don't even think of going after that man, Frank Stainbank, do you hear me?" his wife warned him. "You touch him and you'll hang and where would that leave us? So get it out of your mind. I mean it. Our Kate's in a state as it is, don't you be on her conscience."

Kate was surprised to see her father cowed at his wife's words as he mumbled his agreement, though his hands were in tight fists. Well, that was a first. She had always thought her father was law in the house but realised it was her mother who kept everyone in check.

Frank Stainbank Snr sank back in his chair, his temper temporarily abated as he looked at his daughter. He'd heard what had happened to her and the broken pots, of course he had, and had never trusted Mr Woodman. The man was a weasel, the worst kind of weasel. He wanted Kate to stay out of his way and told her so. Kate reached out her hand to him which he held tightly in his gnarled fingers. She didn't want to go to work and face anyone, she was too embarrassed. She'd be relieved when Mr Roth returned to the pottery.

Her Saturday shift was over and Kate was going to try and forget about it but the episode had put all thoughts of Ted Williams out of her mind.

The last market before Christmas would normally have the females rushing out for the last minute bargains but Kate couldn't face the crowds so she promised to do some baking while the others were out. She found it cathartic making pastry for pies and tarts before mixing, beating eggs and adding flour for cakes. For a short while she was content in the kitchen, Mr Stainbank in the other room by the fire, that was until her eldest brother Frank walked in, bringing not only the cold air but a feeling of despair, as it always was with him.

"Hello, how's my troublesome sister? Caused any damage to property lately?" He laughed loudly.

"Shut up, Frank."

He continued laughing. "It's nice to know I'm not such a bad apple, not the only black sheep of the family. Well, at least I haven't been caught for my misdemeanours. Reverting to type after you did all that running about for me years ago."

"Why don't you shut your mouth," Kate replied. She still felt raw and emotional over what had happened. Picking up a cup, she threw it toward him but it landed just past his shoulder, smashing to the floor.

"You'll have to have that temper knocked out of you if you're going to find yourself a husband," Frank sneered.

"Aye but you won't be doing it, lad, now either keep a civil tongue in your head while you're in this house or get out." Mr Stainbank stood in the doorway.

"I'm the innocent party here. She threw the cup. Needs to curb her emotions," Frank said, picking up his cap.

"On your way out for some more dodgy dealings, are ye, lad?" He looked at his eldest son.

"That's for me to know. Now there's my keep though I don't get much for it." He slapped the money on the table. "I'd be better in a boarding house, so think on," he snarled.

"It's your choice, lad. Yer old enough to make up your own mind but don't be mentioning it to yer mother before Christmas. Let's not spoil it now."

Once the door closed on Frank, Mr Stainbank turned, picking up the coal scuttle. "I'll bank the fire up ready for the horde's return," he laughed.

"Aye," was all she could say. Was that what people were thinking? That she was a criminal breaking all those pots. It hadn't been her fault. Oh, their Frank always knew how to cause trouble. She swept up the broken cup before filling the kettle ready for the others' return. The pastry was cooling and the cakes were in the oven. She would help Rachel and Alice ice them before helping to wrap their presents once they were in bed. She had to keep busy then she wouldn't have time to think.

THE WHOLE FAMILY sat around the table on Christmas Day, including Frank, who also had a few days' holiday from whatever he did. He remained in his bed while the others went to church, apart from Mr Stainbank. He was in charge of keeping an eye on the piece of beef slow roasting in the bottom of the oven. Kate hadn't really wanted to go but it seemed churlish to make a fuss. What she really needed was to shake herself out of this malaise. She had never felt so low before. It was a sort of blackness, like a murder of brooding crows on a washing line.

CHAPTER 6

By the time she returned to work in the new year of 1882, Kate was in a much happier place even though she had seen or heard nothing from Ted Williams, and decided it was probably for the best. The days went quickly with everyone talking about the holiday festivities.

Miss Waller went into a meeting with Mr Roth to discuss future projections but came back with news that Dotty had passed her exams and that Kate could start hers under her friend's tutelage which thrilled them both. Kate was determined to make a go of it to make something of herself and decided there was nothing to stop her eventually being in charge, though she certainly didn't say it, not wanting to alienate herself.

Days went into weeks, into months as Kate's mood became lighter along with the improved weather. Spring saw the snows melting and flowers trying to push through the hard earth. A new life smiling up toward the weak sun. It gave her a feeling of well-being. She was also happy for her brother John who at fifteen was becoming a young man. He was very fond of a young lady named Ellen who had been in the same class through school. Her family seemed happy with the situation as did his. Kate was a little jealous that his life already seemed to be mapped out for him but he was such a kind lad that she didn't resent it too much.

One evening he brought home a leaflet advertising Fossett's Circus which was due in town over the Easter holidays. He chatted to Kate about it, thinking it would be nice if they paid for Rachel and Alice so they could go as a family. She thought it was a great idea especially when her parents said they wanted to come along. She invited Lydia Palmer and John asked Ellen. The ladies in the finishing room were all going so it seemed it would be quite a crowd.

The Stainbanks and entourage bought ninepenny tickets which they hoped would give them a good view. They thought the threepenny ones would be right at the back while the two shilling ones were far too expensive. They also decided to go on the Saturday evening so no one would have to get up for work the following day. Rachel and Alice were almost sick with excitement as Mr Stainbank pretended he wasn't quite ready. John and Kate set off first, John to call for Ellen while Kate was to collect Lydia. They would all meet up at the park gates to walk to the waste ground at the other side where the big top had been set up. There were people everywhere. It seemed the whole of Middlesbrough had come out to see the entertainment.

The ringmaster was dressed in a top hat, a blue jacket with silver buttons shining brightly, his red and white striped trousers tucked into black boots. He carried a whip which he kept throwing so it made a cracking noise. They looked up to the roof as acrobats swung themselves backwards and forwards, being caught before returning to the platform. There was also a tight rope walker who wobbled to the oohing and ahhing. They watched, enchanted, at the horses going round the ring while men and women threw themselves all over them. Dwarves dressed as clowns came round in carts, pretending to throw water at people. The whole crowd laughed and cheered as they watched the evening entertainment.

Kate felt someone's eyes were on her though she couldn't be sure. She looked across the circus ring, spotting Ted Williams. Even when she put her head down, she could feel his stare. Each time she looked through her fringe toward him, he retained eye contact. She didn't want to look but couldn't help herself. Glancing slowly, she pretended to point things out to Alice who was by now sitting on her lap. What was wrong with her? He had never shown any further interest but she had never felt this way about anyone and really didn't know how to deal with it. Her heart skipped a beat every time she looked toward him.

They watched when camels were brought in, then a dancing bear before the dwarfs came back in with a cannon, one poor soul sent into the air to land in a net. The evening culminated in everyone going around the ring as the audience clapped and cheered, standing for an ovation. They all agreed it had been a wonderful evening and well worth the money. Kate looked over to where Ted had been but she couldn't see him. Damn, she thought, damn that man.

It was again a talking point during the week but Kate never mentioned Ted even when Dotty told her that Wyn and his friends had been there. She pretended she hadn't noticed, thinking that was for the best.

The following Saturday, Kate took her sisters to the market to spend their money as usual, and life seemed to get back into a routine quite quickly. There was a stall selling second hand clothes and she spotted a deep blue velvet dress which she thought she could alter to fit. She had wanted some new clothes but didn't have anywhere to wear them but the colour was lovely. It was more than she wanted to pay but it would cheer her up if she bought it and she could always wear it for church. Paying the money quickly, she rounded up the girls so she could get home before she changed her mind.

As they approached the back door, Kate could hear her father laughing loudly, the dulcet tones of Ted, her Ted, telling him some tale. It was too late to try and tidy her hair and wipe her boots as the girls had rushed into the kitchen. Ted stood and she looked at him, then the table where there was a bottle of stout. Both had a glass full of the ale.

"Here she is, the young lady in question," Mr Stainbank said as she put the basket down, removing her coat and bonnet.

"Hello, Ted." Her voice was little more than a squeak and she cleared her throat before saying, "What are you doing here?" Her face flushed with embarrassment.

"This young man has come to ask my permission to take you out for tea next week. He's even organised a chaperone. What do you think of that?"

"That's nice," was all she could say.

"Are ye going to accept the lad, missy," her father roared with laughter. "You're a dark horse, my girl. You never mentioned this un."

Ted finished his beer, saying, "I'd better be off, so will you meet me at the park on Saturday? Miss Palmer will be with us. About three? Would that be alright for you?"

She couldn't speak, her mouth had gone dry so she nodded as her sisters giggled.

"Show Mr Williams out the front door, Kate," Mr Stainbank said, raising his glass.

Ted took her hands in his and although she wanted to pull away in case anyone saw, she didn't. She desperately wanted him to kiss her, but he didn't, putting his lips to her ear instead saying, "Until Saturday, Kate. May I call you Kate?" He smiled and like an idiot she just nodded again as he walked off down the road.

The rest of the day was a blur to her as all thoughts of Mr

Woodman had gone out of the window while Ted had now regained centre stage in her mind. She kept thinking she had nothing to wear other than her Sunday dress. She wouldn't have time to alter and wash the one she had just bought. She made a mental note that if Ted asked her out again, and she hoped and prayed he would, she would spend some of her savings on new shoes and maybe even a new coat and bonnet but she was getting ahead of herself.

By the Saturday morning, Kate could hardly contain herself and was having trouble concentrating on her work. It was so hard not to say anything though she was grateful to her friend Lydia for keeping her secret, just for now as she couldn't stand the teasing. As soon as the hands of the clock reached two, she almost ran home to get washed and changed. She really wanted to make a good impression.

John walked with her to meet Ted and Lydia at Albert Park entrance. Ted Williams was already entrancing her friend. He offered his arms to the two ladies which they linked as though it was the most natural thing in the world. He chatted happily to them both, though if anyone had questioned her later she would not be able to recount a single word he had said. Lydia saw an empty bench where she said she would sit. They could come back for her before they went for tea in the park cafe.

When they were walking alone, Ted stopped his chatter and Kate took up the conversation. She didn't want him to think she had nothing in her head. She was liberal about what she told him about breaking the pottery, but he roared with laughter when she showed him how her arm had caught on Mr Woodman's braces as she fell backwards.

They continued along the pathways, saying hello to one or two other couples who were doing the same, strolling through the park. When they took Lydia for a cup of tea, Kate couldn't stop grinning. Lydia thanked them for their company, saying that it was a relief to get out of the house and away from her mother for a short while but she really should be getting back. Kate realised that this was the end of her first date but knew, she just knew, that it wouldn't be the last as Ted seemed as smitten as her.

Finally on the Monday morning, it was Kate rather than Dotty who was full of what had gone on over the weekend. The whole day she had a warm glow when she thought of Ted and what was more encouraging was that her father seemed to have been taken with him. She didn't want to rush anything, after all it was early days and she was only sixteen, almost seventeen, but she was so excited at the prospect of being able to say she was walking out with Ted.

Kate continued to push herself hard in her work. She wanted to prove she was good enough to put together a portfolio using the colours of the seasons. Spring was full of yellow daffodils and primroses, gentle snowdrops and bluebells. Summer showed large petal roses and sweet peas that you could almost smell off the page. Autumn was Michaelmas daisies with an orb yellow centre, and its fine green leaves were a wonderful contrast to the fragile white petals which she shaded. Winter was full of bright red berries and the greens of holly and fir, with the white pearls of mistletoe.

Dotty was pleased her protege was doing so well, though envious that Kate's work was better than her own. The others were also complimentary, as was Mr Roth, who was back in charge of the pottery. Mr Woodman had returned to Stafford and another pottery which was a great relief for Kate, who was happy she didn't have to worry about him anymore and could concentrate on Ted, her Ted.

However, her relationship with Ted was not so straightforward. His position in the steelworks meant he worked various shifts so wasn't always around when Kate was at home. Sometimes he would call at the house as he finished work on a Saturday when they would walk to the market with Rachel and Alice. Very occasionally, he would be invited to Sunday lunch with the family but Kate found the whole event just too embarrassing and she was unable to speak without blushing.

Sometimes, weather permitting, they would go on a picnic with his friends including Dotty and Wyn, and other times it would be to a concert. His friends seemed to accept that they were a couple which made her feel quite grown up. As time went on, Kate became more and more fond of Ted, his laugh, his easy manner, that his voice seemed to sing as he spoke. To tell the truth, her heart ached for him. She was smitten though she wasn't sure how he felt about her and was too afraid to ask. For her seventeenth birthday, he gave her a brooch, and it was pretty if a little old fashioned, but Kate loved it because Ted had chosen it for her.

CHAPTER 7

Suddenly and without warning, Ted Williams seemed to disappear though Kate said nothing. He would be busy working, she told herself but then doubts began to creep into her mind. She didn't want to ask Dotty about Ted. She was a gossip and surely if she knew anything, she would say so.

What if he was ill? He lived in a boarding house in South Bank near where he worked but it was a place she had never been to. Her father began ribbing her, asking if they had fallen out and she felt she couldn't bear it if they had. The truth was she didn't know what she had done if they had but the gnawing pain in her heart grew bigger and hurt more as the days progressed.

By the Friday evening, Kate was beside herself with worry. She knew her parents would refuse to let her go to his lodgings so she talked to John who was also against the idea, only relenting when she agreed they could go after work on the Saturday. Both agreed to say they were going to look for a present for Ellen for her birthday.

As they walked from the village to the town centre to get a tram, John tried to talk Kate out of her folly. It wasn't done for a woman to chase a man. What would she do if Ted didn't want to see her?

"At least I'll know. My heart is breaking, John. It's a real pain in my breast. I need to know," she said.

They asked the tram driver if he would let them know when to get off for Napier Street. They turned out of town and toward the river where the houses disappeared behind them. She watched the steelworks stretch out before them, belching smoke into the air. The tram filled up with men finishing their shift, the masses walking wearily down the road, their boots sounding like thunder. Seemingly in the middle of nowhere, a row of small terraces appeared.

"You need to get off here, miss," the driver shouted.

John asked one of the men who had got off the bus with them where the street was and he pointed in the right direction. The streets looked the same, back to back tiny houses, and soon they were stood outside number 11.

Kate took a sharp intake of breath before knocking on the door, wishing she was somewhere else.

The woman who answered looked both Kate and John up and down before saying, "I don't take no couples."

"No, no, we are not looking for a room, we are looking for a friend of ours, Ted Williams. Is he here?" Kate tried to keep her voice calm.

"If 'e were a friend of youse, you'd know 'e aint 'ere." The woman was about to shut the door.

John pushed against it. "My sister is worried about him so would be grateful if you could tell us his whereabouts."

The woman looked at Kate before opening her mouth again. "Took yer down as 'e, left yer with a bairn in ye belly? Yer won't be the first nor the last," she chuckled.

"No, he hasn't. What do you take me for? I'm worried as a friend that something has happened to him but I can see we are getting nowhere here. Come on, John." Kate grabbed her brother's arm.

"A lass looking for a bloke means only one thing round 'ere, only means one thing. Try is 'ome in Wales. He's gone there and won't be coming back in 'ere. I've already let 'is room." The woman now managed to push the door shut which was just as well as Kate fell against it. Taking her arm, John led her back to the main road for the tram.

"I'm sure there's an explanation for him going," he said, more to pacify his sister who was shaking as they walked.

"Well, why didn't he let me know. Someone could have passed a message on?" Kate felt foolish having dragged John with her. "I feel such an idiot letting myself be taken in by him. He seemed such a lovely person. I'm so naive in the way of relationships. I was happy with him even though he was my first boyfriend and older than me. I thought him so handsome. Don't tell anyone, John, please. I couldn't bear it."

"Of course not, why would I? But if I ever see him again, I'll give him what for. He won't look so pretty then."

"Oh, John, what would I do without you?" She tried to smile but it didn't reach her eyes. Putting her arm through John's, they walked back the way they came to wait for the next tram to Middlesbrough.

KATE WAS glad to sit on the tram. She thought her legs would give way under her. She was confused over her relationship with Ted. Well, whatever it was, it seemed to be over. She desperately wanted to talk to someone to ask if it was normal to go weeks without any contact. She couldn't talk to her mam, too embarrassing, and Rachel was too young. So that really left Dotty or Lydia, though neither seemed suitable. She didn't know if Lydia had ever had a beau so talking to her could be insensitive. Dotty on the other hand was a gossip who would tell Wyn who would then talk to Ted.

Reading her novels were no help as the heroine always

got the man in the end. They always seemed to confront the man they loved but Kate wasn't so brave to do that, even if she knew where Ted was. It didn't seem fair that men were in charge of everything while women were only good for looking after the home and children. So Kate said nothing but cried herself silently to sleep each night which only made her tired and tetchy during the day. All the worry was making her look pale and insipid. She had little energy. This wasn't how life was supposed to be, but then she thought, why not? Who made the decisions which affected her life? She had always assumed it was God's will to do as he saw fit but now she was beginning to challenge that idea, in her mind anyway. How could he know what was best for her if she didn't know herself?

In the end, the matter with Ted got the better of her so she did ask Dotty how she had started courting Wyn.

"We was just friends at first but then I gave him the big cow eyes, listened to him as though his words were the most important, you know, laugh at his stupid jokes. Then when he's smitten, you know, I pretended I was in a huff with him but gave no clue as to why. Oh, he soon came running when I started chatting to one or two others. Then when he didn't know if he was Cain or Abel, smack." Dotty banged the desk, making them all jump. "I had him in the palm of my hand."

Well, Kate thought, that wouldn't be happening with Ted. She had no control over that but she did have over her employment. She would put all her energy into gaining her diploma and try to put her experience with Ted out of her mind which she knew would be difficult, though in time she may forget him.

Life became mundane for Kate, work, church and little else for six weeks. Forty two days since she had seen Ted. Not that she was counting, oh no, but she was dreading Dotty mentioning the next concert as she knew Lydia would want to go. Perhaps she could ignore Ted if she went but didn't know if she could be as wily as Dotty, nor would she feel confident enough to talk to other men. She tried not to involve herself in the conversation but knew Dotty would start asking questions, questions she couldn't answer.

She was in the kitchen washing the pots when there was a knock on the front door which had them all looking at each other.

Eventually there was a further louder knock. John took the few steps and opened the door. It was Ted. Should he be invited in? Kate looked at her father, shaking her head but could say nothing. She didn't want to see him, not when everyone would be earwigging into their conversation. She didn't know if she could face him so he was sent away.

Mr Stainbank ribbed her, saying, "Ave you fallen out with that nice young man, lass?" but stopped when he saw tears in her eyes.

Kate said little when they sat round the table in the evening. At least if Ted had told her face to face that it was the end of their relationship, she would have coped somehow.

IT WAS as they were walking out of the factory together on the Saturday afternoon that she spied Ted waiting, looking sheepish. John moved closer to her, taking her arm.

"Get her home, lad. Leave this to me," her father said, stepping between them and Ted.

Kate kept her head down, hoping not to have eye contact with the man she knew she loved and hated at the same time. She hurried John along, wanting to find the safety of the house, to be able to put a closed door between them, and at the same time wondering what he had to say for himself.

Leaving the explanations to John, she removed her coat

and bonnet, making her way up the narrow stairs, flinging herself on her bed to listen for her father's return. She strained her ears for what seemed like hours but Mr Stainbank was only a few minutes behind her. Kate heard him talking to the others who would all be sitting, waiting for a bite to eat. The stairs creaked as feet were placed on each one. She didn't want to talk to anyone so she closed her eyes, opening them quickly when her father spoke.

"Listen, lass, your young man has explained to me what happened and I believe him. Go and hear it for yourself and if you want him to leave, I'll put him out meself."

"I can't, dad, what can I say? I feel so stupid."

"Don't say anything then, just listen. Come on." He held his hand out for her.

She tried to smooth down her hair before wiping her eyes. "I must look awful," she sobbed.

"You'll always be beautiful to me, lass," he replied as he went down the stairs in front of her.

They all looked at her as she reached the bottom stair. Her father opened the door to the front room, closing it behind her. Ted stood but she couldn't look at him nor could she speak so just remained where she was. She let him take her arm to sit side by side on the sofa. He kept his hand on hers as he spoke.

"Kate, I am so sorry for your distress. I seem to have hurt you and that was never my intention. I thought I would only be away for a few days. I got word that my father had been taken ill so I rushed to get the train back to Wales."

"You could have written to me or got word somehow," Kate whispered.

"Yes I could, but when I got to my parents my father was in a worse state than I expected. My mother needed looking after. I should have made time, but I thought I would be back. Then my father died, and well, there was the funeral to sort out."

"Oh Ted, I am so sorry for your loss. I didn't know." Kate took his hand.

"No one knew, up here anyway, then once that was over, I couldn't leave my mother on her own. You do see that, don't you? She couldn't cope. Well, anyway, I did some work at Port Talbot steelworks but knew I would have to return here so I brought her, my mother, back with me and we are renting a house the other side of the cemetery."

"When did you get back?" Kate asked, looking at him.

"The day I called here and you wouldn't let me in." Ted smiled. "I'd left mother sorting out the house but I had to see you. I couldn't leave her on her own. You do see that, don't you? I couldn't afford to pay rent on two houses." Ted looked into her eyes.

"I'm sorry for your loss, Ted. I really feel such a child for not believing in you. Can you forgive me for thinking the worst of you?" Kate didn't give him chance to reply before continuing. "I went to your lodgings in case you were ill."

His laugh lit up his face. "You met the landlady. I bet that was an interesting conversation. She doesn't like people, only the money they bring in." His laugh was so deep and rich that she couldn't help but join in.

"Aye, she thought John and I were a couple. 'I don't take no couples'…" Kate tried to say it in the woman's gruff voice, making them both laugh even louder.

Leaning into each other, Ted kissed her gently at first as their arms went round each other.

"I love you, Kate Stainbank," he said quietly.

"I love you, Ted Williams, but what will our families say?" Kate asked, putting her head on his shoulder.

"My mother will love you, I'm sure of that. I think your father likes me so I am sure I can charm your mother and sisters."

"You'll not be charming anyone, Mr Williams. You should have eyes only for me." Kate tried to say it with humour.

"Come on, let's tell them we are still friends. I'm sure they have been straining to hear our conversation."

As Kate took Ted's hand, they opened the door.

"Is there room for another one?" she said.

John grinned at her while her Mr Stainbank shook Ted's hand. As tension was lifted, they all began to talk at once.

Kate finally felt she could breathe out. The rainbow was back in her life, a life that was now set with Ted. The next hurdle would be meeting his mother which would come around sooner than expected as they were invited for dinner the next Sunday Ted was available so she could meet the whole family.

Kate's mood lifted with the return of Ted and it showed in her work at the pottery. Gone were the muted browns and greens, in were the pinks, red and gold. Her only concern now was whether his mother would like her, but with Ted on her side she was hopeful.

A few weeks after her relationship with Ted was back on track, he came for Sunday lunch with his mother.

She wasn't anything like Kate imagined. Ted looked nothing like her. She didn't have the humour or mischief in her eyes. She was a short round woman, hair pulled quite severely into a bun on top of her head, so tight it made her eyes slant. There was powder on her face and her cheeks rosy from the short walk.

After the introductions by Ted, they all sat round the table for lunch, everyone in the Stainbank house on their best behaviour.

Kate didn't immediately warm to this woman. She seemed austere, as though she was looking down on them. She switched language which Ted translated, and Kate was sure he didn't do it word for word.

Over the next few weeks and months, Kate tried to befriend Mrs Williams but the truth was she was a little afraid of her. Ted encouraged Kate to visit his mother on a

Saturday afternoon when he was at work. She made the mistake of taking her sisters but they just sat there and the silence was painful. Mrs Williams made tea and griddle scones but apart from please and thank you, the girls said nothing.

The house was spotless, everything in its place, not like theirs which was clean but untidy with so many in the house. This was to the point of fussy with antimacassars on the backs of the sofa and chairs in the living room, lined up as though on parade.

Kate thought about her own mother who worked hard keeping their place as clean as possible but with all the washing and cooking on the table every night, it was never ending. To her, it was a place which was comfortable whereas this one, she was afraid she would ruffle the chair covers. It was always a relief to say goodbye.

Kate wasn't sure how she would fit in once she married Ted. She would have to give up her job so would be in Mrs Williams' company all day, probably treading on her toes.

CHAPTER 8

KATE 1886

Just weeks after her twenty-first birthday, Kate Stainbank became Mrs Kate Williams. Her dress was a pale cornflower blue but the sleeves were old fashioned, and they were unpicked to be replaced with a fine lace which was also stitched around the hem. The sash around her waist and the ribbons fastening her straw bonnet were a deep rich royal blue. She was the first in the family to wed so they wanted it to be a happy event.

They didn't need much for the house as Ted had already furnished it but Kate wanted something new so over the months bought material to make new bedding. She would sit in the evenings, hemming the material with small neat stitches while Mrs Stainbank embroidered pillow cases. A new eiderdown was made from any pretty material she could find to make a patchwork topping.

The wedding had started off as a small affair where the reception would be held in the Stainbank's house but it seemed almost everyone in Middlesbrough had been invited.

The months leading up to the wedding had Kate in a spin. Every time she saw Ted, he had invited someone else, telling her that one more wouldn't make any difference.

It became obvious that they wouldn't all fit in the small house so the idea to hire a room seemed the solution. Kate had suggested the church hall but Ted laughed, telling her that the Welsh couldn't have a wedding without a beer or two to celebrate the happy couple.

He suggested that he would speak to Mr Oliver at the Albert Park Public House to see if they could rent the room where concerts were held. This was agreed on the promise that all drinks would be purchased from the bar, though they could provide their own food.

Mr Stainbank paid for two barrels of beer while Ted paid for another and sherry or tea for the ladies.

The days before were a hive of activity in the Stainbank house as they baked pies and tarts for the reception so by the morning of the wedding, the whole place was in an uproar, buttering bread for sandwiches. Women were everywhere, trying to get their hair done to the point where Mr Stainbank took John for a walk. Frank was out somewhere but promised to be back in time for the wedding.

Kate hadn't seen Ted for some days due to his work and entertaining of his mother's brother and wife who had arrived from Wales a few days before, and were staying with them.

Rachel and Alice were bridesmaids with small posies of cornflowers to match Kate's dress.

Soon the house was quiet and it was only Kate and her dad, waiting for the carriage to return to take them to the church.

"There's still time to change your mind, lass," Mr Stainbank said, his voice shaking.

"Oh, dad," Kate laughed nervously. "I've never been more sure in my life. I'm so lucky to be marrying Ted."

"He's the lucky one, lass. You look beautiful, but then you've always been beautiful to me."

"Don't, dad, you'll have me crying and I can't have that,

can I?" Kate tried to laugh but just wished she could get the ceremony over. She hated being the centre of attention.

Taking her arm, the two of them walked out to the pavement at the front of the house. The neighbours were out in force, the cheering deafening as she was helped up the step into the carriage.

If you had asked Kate later about the wedding ceremony, she would have looked blankly as it went by as if in a dream. She seemed to wake up as she took Ted's arm and walked back down the aisle as husband and wife, leaving the usher to pay the vicar and collect the marriage certificate.

She remembered more about the very raucous wedding reception at the Albert Park Hotel where the room had been decorated with white and blue garlands. A bar had been opened in one corner, food arranged on tables to the side. Seating was dotted around the room in front of the main table which had a white tablecloth over it.

Everyone was given a drink as they walked into the room to toast the happy couple and once the speeches were over, food and drink flowed. What she would always remember most was when the Welsh began the singing. It filled the whole room and made her quite tearful. She had been brought into this family of proud people and she was glad, glad that they retained their identity, glad that she had met Ted, her Ted.

The happy couple left the reception later than expected as everyone was having such a good time but they didn't have far to go. They were staying in the hotel for two nights before returning to Ted's home. It would be Kate's home now where she would spend more time with his mother than her husband but she was determined to make it work, to make it a happy house for her husband to come home to.

She should never have worried about the wedding night. Her husband was kind and gentle as he slowly undressed her. Inhibitions and passion took over from the kissing which became more demanding. Kate cried out with a mixture of pain and pleasure as he took her as his wife.

They fell asleep in each other's arms. When Ted reached for her the next morning, she found herself enjoying their love making, letting herself be led to a climax.

For the first few weeks, Kate and her mother-in-law walked on egg shells, trying to find a pecking order in the house.

Kate was happy to let her take a role in what to cook for Ted, after all she knew what he liked. All the wedding presents needed to find a home but when Kate tried to move something, Mrs Williams replaced it, mumbling under her breath in Welsh. They had been given a pair of vases from the Linthorpe Pottery, the first ones to be passed off as her own work. However, Kate stood her ground and a peace of sorts ensued. Kate was fortunate that when her temper was about to get the better of her, she could take herself off to see her mother. The Stainbank house was always a place where she could relax and be herself and was always welcome.

A few months after Kate had settled into her new home, she thought she had a stomach bug, feeling queasy, especially in the mornings so she was delighted to realise she was pregnant. It brought a happy truce with her mother-in-law who was keen to help. The pregnancy progressed well. After the first few months of sickness, Kate often found herself with her hands on her belly as the baby kicked.

When she went into labour, she sent Ted for her mother, who told her it would be hours yet, and it was. The bed was prepared, water on the boil and clean towels on the end of the bed as she paced up and down. She was still struggling as the weak morning light came through the curtains to welcome a new day.

"I can't stand it anymore," she groaned as another contraction came.

"There's only one way out, girl," Mrs Williams said in her gruff way.

Kate wanted to laugh hysterically but pushed hard and after twenty hours labour she gave birth to a son, her and Ted's son. Ted finally joined them, saying his son would be named Edward after his father.

Kate was thankful that he seemed a contented child and after three weeks of lying in, she was glad to get some kind of normality back in her life. No one was more delighted than Mrs Williams who had fetched and carried during this time, bringing beef broth to stop her becoming anaemic. The smell of it made Kate's stomach roll. Mrs Stainbank came over most days once she had got everyone out of the house for the day, to help with the washing and nurse her first grandchild.

The first Sunday Ted was off work, the whole family, except Frank, came over to wet the baby's head. They didn't stay long because Kate became tearful when she watched her father holding Edward.

Once she had fully recovered, Kate had a routine with the washing and cleaning while caring for Edward. Mrs Williams was happy to do the cooking so they didn't get in each other's way.

A couple of days a week she would push Edward in his pram to her family home and walk with her mam around the market in the village. She stopped to talk to people she hardly knew who wanted to look at her baby. It gave her time away from her mother-in-law who she knew was glad of the quiet time.

Her life seemed set into a routine, some might say mundane, but she loved it. She wasn't sure she would want five children like her mother but was happy to let nature take its course.

PART II

CHAPTER 9

RACHEL STAINBANK AGED 14, MIDDLESBROUGH 1886

Rachel had moved to Middlesbrough with her family without too much fuss and ado. She had settled in quickly, making friends. She had a lot of friends. No one really noticed her growing up, apart from the fact that she had grown mouthy, challenging not only her mother but also her father. Rachel in a way was a softer version of Frank except she didn't have his dark side. She didn't mind questioning her parents with the whys and why nots when she didn't get her own way. It seemed at times that she liked the confrontation, to push the boundaries as far as she could. Sometimes it was the little things like playing in the ginnell for that extra few minutes after she had been called in. Other times she could disappear for hours, going off to Albert Park or the market on a Saturday morning with some of the other girls in the street. It didn't matter to her that she would have to come straight home from school for a week to do chores because she had done what she wanted.

The family were very surprised when Rachel came home with a hundred per cent in her school certificate, much to Kate's chagrin that she hadn't managed it herself. Rachel was flippant about it as though she had expected no less.

Her father said he would speak to Mr Roth to see if he could find her a position and the whole house went quiet when she said no, she didn't want to work there. She wasn't going to hang onto his coat tails like Kate or John and she wasn't giving up on her dream like Kate. She was going to be a nurse. The family were surprised as no one knew she had a dream, or where had the idea come from. It wasn't the kind of thing nice girls did, more spinsters who found themselves without means, her parents told her in different ways.

Mr Stainbank told her that she had to the end of the school holidays to find a job because she needed to bring money into the house. It didn't faze her like it had Kate. Rachel was very confident that a job would be found, more to the point one she would find for herself.

On the Monday morning, those in work had already left, leaving Rachel, Alice and their mam in the house. Rachel put on her Sunday dress before picking up Kate's best bonnet.

"That's your sister's," Peggy Stainbank said.

"Aye well, she ain't wearing it and she won't know if you don't tell er," Rachel replied as Alice giggled.

"What's wrong with yours?"

"Yer know what's wrong with mine. It belonged to God knows who afor I got it and the ribbon don't know what colour to be."

"Don't you take God's name in vain in this house, missy. Anyway, where you off to?" Peggy Stainbank raised her voice.

"Thanks for asking. I'm doing what dad told me, looking for a job. Now I may be out sometime, or not, is that alright?" Rachel said in a condescending manner.

"Away with yer then and let me get on." Mrs Stainbank flapped a cloth toward her.

Rachel, in a fit of pique, went out by the front door, slamming it hard, making the glass in the window frame rattle in her wake. She had stepped straight out onto the pavement with her shoulders back and head held high but now she was outside, she really didn't know where to go.

Some of her school friends had found jobs in the big houses but only because they knew someone who already worked there. They would live in and skivvy for a pittance and she didn't want to do that on both counts. For all her bravado she wasn't ready to leave home and certainly wasn't going to spend her life on her knees, scrubbing floors or fireplaces of houses she would never be able to afford.

Her only thought was to go and ask in the shops in the village where they might know someone who needed a carer. She didn't want to be a nursemaid or a nanny because she didn't like children, already deciding she would never have any of her own. She had this idea in her mind that she would be something between a companion and a nurse for a lady who was getting on in years and really needed company. That was her dream and she wasn't giving up on it like Kate had with her teaching. She was no fool, that's for certain, she said to herself.

Rachel wasn't sure where to start, thinking that perhaps she should have thought about it more. Writing out a note to leave with people would have been a start but no matter. She was determined to go home with something, an interview or even the name of someone who might know a family who could offer her a job.

Her first thought was to try the apothecary. They might know someone so she pushed the door open, listening to the tinkling of the bell. Rachel started her conversation with the man in his white coat standing behind the counter who looked at her over his glasses while shaking his head. It was the same story in the other shops she tried. No one could help her.

She was downhearted, really not wanting to admit defeat so as a last resort she walked into the post office. They couldn't help but suggested she put a note in their window at a penny for four weeks. With nothing to lose, she accepted the piece of card and pencil while thinking what to write.

POSITION WANTED
School Leaver seeks position as companion/nurse. To live out. Wages negotiable. Please contact in first instance Miss Rachel Stainbank care of the Post Office.

THE LAST PART she had written on the advice of the post mistress. She handed over her penny, saying she would call back in a few days to see if there had been any interest.

She didn't know what to do with herself but as she still had a few pennies left in her purse, she thought she would go to the park cafe and treat herself to a cup of tea rather than go home. Rachel knew she shouldn't walk through the park alone, never mind buy her own drink, but she wanted to be a rebel, wanted to do something for herself. Feeling quite elated at her new found freedom, she walked confidently down the path, neither looking left nor right, enjoying the feeling of freedom.

Ordering herself a pot of tea and a homemade biscuit, she felt very grown up even though it was the money Kate had been giving her each week. She sat herself at a small table by the window, not caring if she was seen. The only other people in the cafe were two well dressed middle-aged women, and a man and woman sitting by the door chatting, though the man looked a little exasperated. Rachel tried not to stare so she looked out of the window and onto the lake.

The waitress brought her tray, asking if she was waiting for someone which Rachel told her no but she had been looking for work now she had left school. They talked generally with her explaining what she was looking for and that she had put a note in the post office. She asked the waitress, who was also the owner, if she knew of anyone but again was told no.

She did say that she would be happy to put a notice in her window but in the meantime if she wanted Saturday work, they would take her on a trial basis. Rachel was delighted, accepting immediately. Come along at eight o'clock, she was told, and bring an apron, though a white cap would be provided. She would receive four pence for the day and a share of any food left over.

Rachel had long since finished her pot of tea but sat watching the few people go by. The other customers left, leaving her with the owner who introduced herself properly as Annie Clifton. It was difficult for Rachel to discern her new employer's age. Annie could have been anywhere between mid twenties to mid forties but was probably somewhere in between. She seemed a canny soul, happy to chat. She told Rachel that her mother did the baking which she brought in each day in an old perambulator which had belonged to a number of nieces and nephews over the years. The hood was now ripped and torn and the brake a little dodgy but it served its purpose.

Miss Clifton, Annie, asked Rachel if she was in a rush to go anywhere and when she shook her head said it would be a good opportunity to show her the ropes while it was quiet. Rachel took off her coat and Kate's bonnet, throwing them on the chair before following Annie behind the counter. She was quick to learn the prices though she would mainly be responsible for clearing tables, taking trays to customers, sweeping the floor and washing up. As it was still quiet, they had another cup of tea. Rachel had the feeling Annie was probably glad of the company. Shaking hands as they parted, Rachel set off for home in a really good mood. The money wasn't much but she could save it until she could find out more about nurse training, if there was such a thing.

The house seemed gloomy and quiet when she returned,

only her mother was about in the yard, bringing in the washing.

"Give me a hand with these sheets, will you, lass?" she said, not looking directly at Rachel.

"Let me get out of me good clothes first," Rachel snapped, "an' if you're interested I've got meself a temporary job." Why was it her family always seemed to rile her and annoy her so much that she always felt ready to snap.

Rachel grudgingly told her mother about her Saturday position and where she had been but knew it wouldn't be enough. They would grind her down until she took any kind of job and she was going to have to keep her wits about her to make sure that didn't happen. As families went, they should be quite well off with the amount of money coming in. After all, her father had always been in work and Frank tipped up money every week. Now Kate and John were working, they should be less frugal with their spending. Her clothes had always been hand-me-downs from Kate though she was now taller. Her and John were tall and slim like their mother while the rest of them had the more stocky build of their father.

All that would change when she had enough money. She would buy her own clothes, colourful ones not the drab serviceable greys and greens. She also wanted a nice pair of boots, leather ones with pointed toes and buttons down the side not the flat lace up working boots she wore now, stuffed with paper and a piece of old leather over the hole in the sole.

Rachel sat in the kitchen, listening to her mother wittering on, thinking the sooner she found herself a proper job and got out of the house the better. She didn't sit and read like Kate, too old to be playing out with Alice and her friends so if she didn't get something soon she would go out of her mind.

By the Thursday of the first week of the school holidays,

Rachel was tearing her hair out so she offered to go and do some shopping. She could call at the post office to see if there had been any developments to her note in the window. Take Alice with you, her mother had said but she didn't want to be a babysitter.

"How can I? If someone has left a note, I may have to go and have an interview. I can't take her, can I?"

"I don't want you going to strange people's houses, our Rachel. You know nowt about 'em." Peggy Stainbank looked at her middle daughter.

"I can look after myself. I'm no fool like our Kate, nor a bairn like Alice. I've grown up or haven't you noticed?" Rachel snapped.

"Don't you take that tone with me, girl. You're not too big for a slap. What'll your father say?"

"Dad say? He won't say nowt, he just wants an easy life and as long as I pay me way, he won't care. He's never done owt about our Frank and his capers, has he?" Rachel was just beginning to get going. "Anyway, where does all the money go, I ask you? I've never had clothes or shoes that haven't been handed down. At this rate, poor Alice will look like a beggar." She jumped back as her mother swiped her arm out to catch her with a slap.

"You won't do that again, mam, I'm telling you. I've a right to say me piece especially once I'm earning so think on." Rachel headed to the door, rubbing her arm.

"You're getting too big for your boots, my girl. While you are under this roof, you'll do as you're told, do you hear? Do you hear?" Peggy shouted.

"Aye, I'm not deaf and half the street will have heard." Rachel shut the door, smiling to herself. She couldn't wait to be earning her own money then they'd see, just wait.

CHAPTER 10

Rachel was surprised that two notes had already been left for her, though they didn't say much other than give their addresses. Deciding to go to the furthest away first, she walked toward the centre of the town. Parcels Yard was close to the railway station and everywhere seemed to be coated in a layer of black soot.

The house was in the middle of a terrace with a Methodist Church at the end of the row. There were snotty nosed bare footed urchins playing in the street where water ran in rivulets at the side of the road. As Rachel knocked on the door, the filthy net curtain fluttered and a man looked directly at her.

"Don't want no do gooders here, be on your way," he shouted.

"It's Rachel Stainbank. You left a message." Rachel realised she was shouting in the street as the children momentarily stopped their game to stare. There was silence. She stood, not knowing whether to knock again or walk away. Standing looking at the children who had returned to their game, she moved from one foot to the other.

The door was opened by a short stocky man with a

mountain of white wispy hair while his moustache and beard were stained yellow from goodness knows what. The smell hit her. It came from the inside to the outside. Rachel wasn't sure what it was... body odour, cigars, damp or cats, or even a combination. The man ushered her in, which she didn't want to do but couldn't just remain where she was. Trying to suck herself in as best she could so she didn't brush the brown walls, she followed him into the gloomy front room. It was cluttered with two single beds, a fireplace and one comfy chair, though comfy stretched the word as the stuffing seemed to be escaping everywhere. Under the window was a table piled with pots, a pan and crockery as well as a number of flies, both dead and alive.

"Who sent yer, miss, and what do yer want?" the man growled.

"You left a note saying you might have a position!" Rachel replied, thinking she could never work here in a million years.

"I never left no message," he replied.

"Well, I've got this note with your address on it," she said, showing him the piece of paper. "It was left at Linthorpe post office."

"Linthorpe, eh! That'll be from ower sister. She's a proper busybody, thinks me and our Charlie can't manage." He looked at her.

"Well, she's quite right, sir. What you need is a bucket of hot water and some carbolic, that should do the trick," she smiled, "and an open window."

He didn't seem to take offence, saying to her, "It will only be a couple of hours a week, missy, that's all we can afford."

"I'm looking for something full time. Sorry I wasted your time." Her shoes which were now stuck to the floor sort of peeled away in a sucking noise which continued to the front door.

Once outside, she took a deep breath before looking at

her shoes to make sure she hadn't brought anything out with her.

Rachel felt sorry for shouting at her mother that morning. They had never, even when she was small, lived in such a terrible place. They had never played out with no shoes on their feet or a filthy face. She might have gone home with one but always had a cloth and water around her face each morning and evening whether they wanted it or not. Their house was always clean as were their clothes, even if they were old and second hand. Rachel reluctantly thought her mam was right about going to places on her own. No one knew where she was and anything could have happened.

Well, it didn't, she said to herself, shaking the thoughts out of her mind as she walked quickly back toward the village, though the smell remained in her nostrils. That was until she reached the second address which was a butcher's shop. It seemed strange to her that they would be looking for someone but waited patiently while a lady was being served some tripe as they chatted, while Rachel stood thinking the smell of meat and sawdust had a better perfume to that of the house. She watched the butcher, his large hands seemingly caressing a piece of meat, but his action swift as he chopped through bone.

Rachel could hear children screaming and yelling somewhere close which seemed to irritate the man. She explained why she was there as he looked her up and down before coming from behind the counter and locking the door which alarmed her.

"The Mrs is upstairs," he said. "Follow me."

Realising the sound of the children was coming from a flat above the shop, she followed the butcher up the stairs where there were three doors off the landing. He opened a door into a bedroom. Rachel looked at the poor woman propped up in the bed, trying to feed a screaming baby. She looked grey and exhausted while three other children were causing mayhem in the small space around the bed.

"Stop it," the butcher's voice boomed, making the baby scream even more, followed by the smallest child who was crawling about at the foot of the bed. "I'll have to get back to the shop," he said apologetically as he turned. Once the door was closed behind him, the other children began jumping around again.

"Be quiet, children. Jack, play nicely with your sisters while I talk to Miss…? I'm sorry, who are you?" the woman said meekly.

"My name is Rachel Stainbank and I'm here about a position." She pulled out the piece of paper.

"Oh yes, that's right but it's only temporary until I get back on my feet. I need someone to look after these three." She nodded at the children. "My mother won't have them, says they are feral but they are just boisterous. Stop it for a minute, will you?" she shouted.

"Oh right," Rachel said. "I have no experience of looking after children." She looked at the poor woman who seemed at the end of her tether.

"I could pay you a shilling a day if you would come in from eight until six but that would include cleaning, washing and preparing meals," the woman told her.

She must be desperate, Rachel thought. A shilling a day was a fortune. "It would only be Monday to Friday." She didn't want to give up the cafe job on the Saturday even though she would be eight pence a week short if she did.

"All right." The woman seemed to fall back on the pillows. "Can you come in tomorrow and I'll pay you for one day, then for the next couple of weeks?"

"Yes, that's fine, Mrs…? What'll I call you?" Rachel was already thinking of the boots with the pearl buttons she would be able to buy.

"Mrs Chapman, this is Jack, Molly and Connie." She waved her hand at the children. "The baby is Winnie."

Rachel thought they looked like little devils and wondered what she had let herself in for. Taking her leave, she went back through the shop, explaining to Mr Chapman that she would be back at eight o'clock the following morning.

Smiling at the thought of five shilling and fourpence a week for the next few weeks, she would be earning more than Kate or John when they first started work. Alright, it was only for a few weeks but she would be able to buy lots of things off the market stall. She wouldn't tell her family exactly how much she was earning. As long as she tipped up something, they didn't need to know. She could already see a lovely blue corded dress and a pair of boots, maybe gloves and a new hat. One step at a time… she would have to tame those children first.

Rachel was thankful that she only worked the Friday of the first week. When she arrived, Mr Chapman already looked at the end of his tether and grateful to be working in the shop. Leaving her coat and hat on the peg in the kitchen, she took the narrow steps to the bedroom where she knocked. She wasn't sure anyone would hear with all the noise so she pushed it open but remained where she was.

Rachel's first day was like a baptism of fire with the children testing her patience to the limit. The two eldest fought incessantly until she smacked them both, making them sit at opposite sides of the fireplace. The look of shock on their faces made her want to laugh, but it worked. The youngest was crawling into everything, whinging and whining all the time for no apparent reason. Mrs Chapman said it was because she still wanted to be on the titty.

The children were still in their nightclothes and after a brief conversation with Mrs Chapman, she took them downstairs for breakfast. She couldn't find anything and with the very smelly baby under her arm, she had to go into the shop to ask for help. Finally with milk warmed and porridge made, Rachel sat feeding the youngest on her knee while the other two used the only clean spoons she could find. Jack began throwing his food around with his sister joining in. Getting up, she closed the door to the shop.

"Right, you two, if you've finished, go and get your clothes." She should have put the kettle on to warm water but never mind they would have to be washed in cold for today.

The only place she could find to put the baby was the perambulator but that would mean the child would be downstairs while Rachel was upstairs cleaning up the living room. She felt that she had taken too much on but didn't have time to reconsider when the other two resurfaced with all sorts of items of clothing.

She muddled through the day and was relieved when she said goodbye to Mrs Chapman, who handed over her shilling, before leaving by the shop, but before she could make her escape, Mr Chapman gave her a package of scrag end. "Great for stew," he told her and she just nodded in agreement. Well, her mother would be happy with that and it gave her an idea. She wouldn't mention the shilling, just tell them it was a day's trial. She was exhausted, going to bed the same time as Alice in the hope she would get some sleep, but her mind went over and over how she could make her life easier for the next few weeks.

RACHEL STOOD WAITING for Annie outside the café, hearing the squeaky wheels of the perambulator before she saw her. They seemed immediately happy in each other's company as they chatted and worked at the same time. Kettles were set to boil, teapots stood with tea leaves ready to be filled with the water. Rachel set out tables while telling Annie about her nightmare the day before. They were both laughing loudly as the sign was turned to open and almost immediately the first of the day's customers came in.

Rachel had thought this would be an easier job and in some ways it was but by the time the sign was turned to closed, her legs and back were aching. School and her school certificate hadn't prepared her for this at all. Just sitting at her desk seemed such an easy way of life now. The morning had been busy with a constant stream of customers in groups, couples and one or two men alone. As she began putting the chairs onto the tables ready to wash the floor, Annie stopped her.

"Come on, stop for five minutes and have a cup of tea. We deserve it." She had filled a plate with a few of the fancies left over. "How's your first day been, and be honest?" She pushed Rachel's arm. "Will you be coming back again or laughing about me with your family?"

"I didn't realise how tired I would be," Rachel replied, "but I've enjoyed it. I must say I'm looking forward to having a sleep in tomorrow and what I'll be like after a full week at the Chapman's, I don't know," and they both laughed.

She walked along the park path to the main gates with Annie before picking up a small bag of cakes from the perambulator and watched as her new friend squeaked off down the road. Rachel was still smiling when she walked into the house with her fourpence wage. She put the cakes and tuppence on the table but her mother gave her it back.

"Here, lass, keep it. You've earned it and you've even brought cakes home."

Rachel took the money back with only a slight feeling of guilt. She had managed with only two days of work to have amassed the grand total of one shilling and fourpence. Alright it wasn't yet a fortune, but it would go toward her nursing course or new clothes. She felt so grown up at last.

. . .

As Mrs Chapman began to feel better, Rachel would sit and talk to her while they were having a drink. She questioned her about childbirth, labour and the after effects but had to hurriedly explain that she wanted to be a nurse, she really wasn't being personal, just interested and it wasn't something she could talk to her mother about.

When the weather was fine, she would take the two eldest to the park to let off steam while the two smaller ones were asleep and Mrs Chapman resting. By the end of the first week, the children were better behaved though Rachel was exhausted. By the end of the fourth week, she had really had enough and realised that she had earned every penny of her wages. She now had more admiration for her mother who had managed to run their home with military precision when they were all small, and the evening meal was always on the table when they got home. Her mother must have had the patience of a saint.

As Mrs Chapman was now up and about, Rachel was pleased to be surplus to requirements. Saying goodbye was easy, her decision to never have children confirmed. Though the guinea she had earned had made it worthwhile, she couldn't have managed permanently. As she left, Mr Chapman thanked her profusely and gave her a string of sausages, a bag of chitterlings and enough minced lamb to make a pie, all wrapped in brown paper.

CHAPTER 11

Rachel had told the family she was earning three shilling a week, agreeing that she would hand over one shilling and sixpence which still left her with fifteen shilling after five weeks, plus one shilling and fourpence from the cafe. The first day she wasn't at work and the market was on, she took herself off to purchase a new pair of boots. The ones she picked were a little tight but nothing some wet newspaper in the toes wouldn't sort out. She would have loved a new dress but didn't want to spend her money too quickly and give the game away, so picked herself two pairs of stockings instead. She would wait until she had a new job before spending any more, saving the rest for her eventual training.

Rachel found she loved working at the little cafe and Annie had become a firm friend. She could talk to her about things she wouldn't dream of talking to her mother about. Although she knew she would have to find another position soon, she was loath to leave Annie, the cafe and the customers.

Continuing to wander around the village to ask about work, Rachel found nothing but decided not to put another notice in the post office window. When she walked to the village, she would often call in at the cafe for a cup of tea to keep out of the house as long as possible. It was just such a day as the autumn wind blew the leaves off the trees and blew her in through the cafe door, that a new opportunity sort of fell into her lap.

The cafe wasn't full but customers drifted in after a bracing walk through the park. Annie was pleased to see her as usual, and Rachel took a seat next to the counter as they chatted between customers. The door was flung open, bringing the cold air rushing in. A gentleman tried to bring a lady in through the door in a bath chair but the door wouldn't quite open far enough so Rachel jumped up to move the table and chairs, helping to bring the lady into the warmth.

The gentleman mumbled his thanks, ordering tea and cake for himself and, Rachel assumed, his wife. She watched him remove the blanket from around her knees before taking off her gloves and pouring their tea. She didn't want to stare, really she didn't, but was fascinated, watching him carefully break the cake into small pieces so his wife could pick them up with her right hand. Her left arm hung limply from her shoulder, hand in her lap which she seemed unable to move. The man talked quietly as the lady nodded or shook her head depending on the answer.

Once the couple left, Rachel put the table and chairs back in place, realising the lady's gloves had fallen to the floor, probably when the blanket was replaced over her legs. Picking up her purse, she told Annie she would see her on Saturday before rushing off to try and find the couple who surely couldn't have got far. Walking quickly to keep out the cold as much as anything, she headed toward the park gates, where she spotted them by the water fountain but couldn't catch the man's eye. Eventually she caught them and handed the gloves over. They walked together where she found them happy to listen to her as she explained that she worked at the cafe on a Saturday but was looking for work until she had enough money to train to be a nurse. The wind was beginning to gust, bringing the rain and as they were about to hurry away, the gentleman, Mr Hylton, asked if she would care to visit his wife the following afternoon, which she agreed.

What a nice man, she thought, as she walked home. He seemed very caring and they lived in a big house in the village so she was looking forward to seeing it. She was vague as to where she had been when her mother asked, just telling her that she should try and get herself out and about a bit more, there was a big world out there. Rachel did feel a little mean but thought how narrow her mother's life was, but then they never talked about what she had hoped for when she was younger.

As Rachel put her coat on the following day, Peggy Stainbank asked, "Where are you off to now?"

"For an interview."

"You never mentioned it. Who's it for? What will you be doing?" Peggy was looking at her middle daughter, not understanding her at all.

"I've got to go or I'll be late. I'll tell you later." Rachel dashed out of the house, knowing she really should try harder to talk to her mother, promising to try to when she got back.

THE HYLTON'S house was set back from the road by a garden that was covered in weeds along with the brown, red and gold leaves which had fallen from the trees and onto the path. The large brass knocker was in the middle of the door. It echoed around the porch as she knocked. Mr Hylton seemed to have been waiting behind the door for her as he opened it immediately, ushering her into the front parlour.

Mrs Hylton was sitting in a chair by the window. Rachel noticed the poor woman's face had dropped at one side, making her smile lop sided, however she had a sparkle in her eyes, a spirit which made Rachel follow suit and smile back.

"May I take your coat, Miss Stainbank? And I'll go and bring a tray in," Mr Hylton said.

"Thank you but please call me Rachel." She smiled widely at the man.

As he went out of the room, Rachel talked to Mrs Hylton about the lovely view she had to watch the world go by. The room itself was cosy, a warm fire, a daybed, a comfy chair next to a bookcase piled high with books and a table with two chairs sitting in the bay window. She continued to talk about the weather, her work at the cafe, anything as Mrs Hylton nodded, listening intently.

Mr Hylton returned after a few minutes and the conversation came mainly through him. They had a young girl who lived in but she wasn't the brightest of buttons, he told Rachel. She tried hard but didn't have the intellect to stimulate his wife and was unable to read. He explained that his wife had been very fortunate that the stroke hadn't killed her and she had improved enormously over the past few months. She still had difficulty on her left side and her speech hadn't come back but she understood everything, even when he swore. He continued to say that his wife's care had been somewhat erratic as their daughter-in-law now had another child to care for, making that three, and his son was training as an estate manager.

Mr Hylton, or Dr Hylton to be correct, said he needed to spend more time at work or it would go to the dogs so how would Rachel feel about coming and helping his wife out? It would be helping with her speech by talking to her and asking her to repeat words. Perhaps reading or even something he had read about, a sort of massage. He wanted

Rachel to encourage his wife to walk and this was where she would need to be strict in making sure it was done regularly.

Rachel had immediately felt comfortable with the couple but had a few stipulations of her own. Firstly, she didn't want to work on a Saturday as she loved being in the cafe and didn't want to let Annie down. Secondly, she didn't want to live in but other than that she was happy to help in whatever way she could and hopefully help Mrs Hylton to get better.

They agreed a wage of three shilling a week which would include lunch, with her hours from eight until five, and she would prepare an evening meal with the girl before she left. Rachel laughed, telling him she didn't have much experience as a cook but would do her best. Her wage would rise after six months if they were both happy. Occasionally she may have to stay late if Dr Hylton was with a patient and Rachel was happy with that. Dr Hylton also told her she could take some of his medical books to read if she really was serious about going into nursing.

So for Rachel her life in the short term seemed set. She would be able to save money for her nurse training but would now be able to dip into her savings for that longed for dress. She couldn't believe how well things had turned out and at least her parents wouldn't complain that she wasn't working.

PART III

CHAPTER 12

ALICE STAINBANK AGED 13, MIDDLESBROUGH 1887

Alice wasn't clever like Kate or Rachel but she was pretty. Her hair was corn yellow with a natural curl, and her eyes green, very pale green. Her face was oval with a nose which turned up just enough to be cute. She had a pleasant nature, eager to please but as the baby of the family she found she could get her own way with her mother. Her father was another matter. He was strict with all his children and to be truthful Alice was a little frightened of him. The only member of the family who took no notice was Frank, and Alice had to admit that she was much more afraid of him than of her father. No one seemed to care that she, being thirteen, was coming up to sitting her school certificate and didn't think she would get very good marks. As no one else seemed interested, neither was she. Alice didn't want to find a job but stay at home and play with her friends.

Frank had sworn her to secrecy when he began meeting her from school. He would just appear out of the shadows where her friends would drift away, making her nervous. John would sometimes meet her if he wasn't working and she didn't have this feeling of foreboding like with Frank.

At first Frank would just walk with her, talking about

nothing really. Then he started bringing her small gifts, a piece of ribbon, a farthing, a small linen bag with a drawstring to put everything in but her favourite was a small butterfly brooch with colourful, some would say gaudy, stones. Alice had longed to pin the brooch on her dress to show off to her friends or wear the ribbon in her hair but Frank said no. It was to be their secret for now, she had to tell no one or he wouldn't bring her anything more. Reluctantly Alice agreed, hiding everything in the bag and placing it under the mattress out of view. They never talked to each other at home but that wasn't unusual as he didn't talk to anyone unless they spoke to him first.

The fact that she had a secret fascinated Alice, making her feel special. She thought she was Frank's favourite but wasn't sure she should be happy about that. She was relieved on the days he didn't meet her but she liked his gifts. Alice desperately wanted a cat, like her friend Bella, whose cat had six kittens. She had picked a small tortoise shell one but her mother had said definitely no, she couldn't have it. She thought if Frank brought it home for her, no one would refuse him so she wanted to ask him next time he met her. She hadn't seen him for a few days and she hoped the kitten wouldn't go to someone else before she had the chance to ask.

Alice was surprised when Frank arrived like an apparition, moving below a small copse of trees across from the school. Striding over to meet her, he slowed his steps to match hers.

"How's school, sis'?"

"Alright. What are you doing here?" Alice asked.

"How would you like a ride in my boss's cab? Come on, it won't take long." Frank put his arm around her shoulder.

"No, I've got to go straight home." Alice tried to pull away but he gripped her shoulder tightly. "You're hurting me. Let go, Frank."

"I'll make sure you get home. You'll be able to see the big house." Frank smiled at her.

"Can I pat the horse?" Alice became excited at the thought.

"Yes, of course you can. I might even find an apple you can give him," Frank replied, steering her toward the corner of the street.

A little way along the road but out of sight of the school was the cab with a grey horse waiting for them. Frank didn't speak but helped her to climb in before tapping on the roof to let the driver know they were ready. She fell back onto the seat as the horse moved off, soon trotting along at a fair speed.

Alice knew she should have gone straight home but the excitement of riding in the cab pushed the thought out of her mind. Neither spoke as they headed away from Linthorpe past Albert Park and onwards. Alice was fascinated, looking in awe at the houses going by in a flash. She had almost forgotten Frank was there until he spoke, making her jump. "When we get to the house, someone will meet you to take you inside to meet my boss."

"Won't you be coming in with me?" Alice became alarmed.

"No, I have work to do. Be nice to the man. He let you ride in the cab, didn't he? Later we can feed the horse. I'll see if I can find that apple if you are really good." Frank was now rubbing his hands together somewhat manically. Alice nodded but was now becoming fearful, wishing she had run away from him and gone home instead, thinking this is what she would do in future but she hadn't asked about the kitten, and she really needed to ask.

The cab stopped and the door was opened almost immediately as Frank stepped out, helping Alice down the steps. The large wooden door at the side of the house was also open. She was ushered into the kitchen which was bigger than the downstairs of their house. She turned as the door was closed firmly behind her but Frank had gone, leaving her looking at the number of people working around the kitchen table. A man came toward her saying, "Follow me!" and they walked through another door into a large hallway, bigger, much bigger, than anything Alice had ever seen. She stopped to marvel at the paintings, tables and even the size of the staircase but was hurried through yet another heavy wooden door. The man ushered her in where she stood looking around the room. It was gloomy with the curtains drawn even though it was still early. At first Alice thought she was alone and thought she might let herself out and go and look for Frank to take her home.

"Come closer. Let me look at you, girl," a voice said. Sitting in a high backed chair to the side of the unlit fire was a man, smoke rising from his cigar which gave the room an eerie feel and the smell made Alice's nose wrinkle.

Alice involuntarily rubbed her laced boots on the back of her stockings before slowly moving forward. She didn't want to go forward and closer to the man, she wanted to go home. He looked huge in the chair with a great bushy beard and mop of greying hair. Even the hand she could see holding the cigar was hairy. She stood staring at him, too frightened to get any closer or to speak. She wanted to leave and leave now but she didn't know what she should do.

"Would you like a glass of milk and an apple?" he said, rising from the chair in a smoky haze. She saw he was quite tall, bigger than her dad, Frank or John.

"Yes, please, Mr." Alice stood closer, taking the glass from his hand. After drinking the milk, she continued to hold the glass, waiting for the man to speak again. Picking up two apples from a fruit bowl on a side table with one hand, he held out his other hand for the glass before passing them to her. Alice didn't like the way he looked at her, just beady eyes looking out from under his bushy eyebrows. Everything about him seemed to be hairy. She didn't speak nor did she hold out her hand because the man frightened her. He looked like a shaggy dog and she couldn't help but stare at him. She couldn't see his mouth move when he spoke.

"There you are, one for you and one for the horse. What is your name, young lady?" he asked.

"Alice, Alice Stainbank. Thank you, sir, but I must go. My mam will be worried about me," she replied, looking around the room for the way out. Her eyes now accustomed to the gloom, she saw numerous ornaments sitting on various tables. How she would have loved to have picked one up to just look, not to take it, but just to look.

"Yes, of course, I have kept you long enough but would you like to visit again and maybe you could stay longer next time. It would be nice to get to know you better."

Alice nodded her head in agreement though she wasn't sure why.

"Good girl. I will make some arrangements then but you must keep it a secret. Can you do that, Miss Stainbank?"

"Can I tell Frank? He's my brother. He brought me and I don't know how to get here myself. He can keep a secret," she told him.

"Yes, of course. I'll talk to him and make arrangements for you to visit again."

Once Alice had left the room, the man said to himself, "Well, well… Frank brought one of his sisters. That's low even for him. He must be desperate to remain in my employ. A pretty little thing though and certainly cleaner than some of the girls Frank brought to the house." The man smirked as he drew deeply on what was left of his cigar, thinking life was good.

Alice stood at the top of the steps, looking down into the yard. The horse and cab were still there as was Frank who was talking to the driver.

"Alright, Alice?" Frank asked as he helped her down the

steps from the kitchen, holding her elbow as her hands were holding the two red apples. He didn't wait for an answer but led her to the horse who was eyeing her. It was bigger than she expected when she got up close but she held out one of her hands. "Put your hand flat, Alice," Frank told her. "Come on, don't be scared. He won't hurt you."

She felt the velvety softness of the horse's nose as he took the apple and although she would have liked to have eaten the other one herself, she held out her hand again.

"Let's get you home before you get into bother. Don't forget, this is our secret. Promise, Alice. Say it!" Frank said to her.

"Promise. The man said I could come again. Can I, Frank?" Alice sounded excited at the thought.

"Alright, I'll let you know. It will be soon so you will have to think of an excuse to be late home from school. Can you do that?" Frank looked at his sister.

"Yes, I can." Alice put her back against the seat, enjoying the ride back into town. Suddenly the fear left her. She had a secret none of her friends could know, but she hugged herself at the thought.

"Where have you been, madam?" her mother asked. "You should have been home from school ages ago."

"I went to Mary's allotment to see the chickens. They are laying eggs and they will be chicks. Can I go and see them again, mam, can I? Pleeease," Alice pleaded.

"We'll see. You should have let me know so I didn't worry. Now, get from under my feet while I finish sorting out tea. Go on with you."

Each day as Alice finished school, she looked for Frank. She hadn't asked him about the kitten and they would be going to new homes Bella had told her. She couldn't ask him when he was in the house at the weekend because they were never alone. The thought of going to the big house scared and excited her at the same time. She desperately wanted to ride in the cab and look around the house but wasn't sure about the man. She had never seen anyone like him but her stomach had butterflies when she thought of him. It made her feel funny.

Her mother had made it clear on more than one occasion that under no circumstances was she getting a kitten, no matter how many times Alice begged. She didn't want it round her feet all day when Alice was at school. It seemed that Frank would be her only hope, so she knew she would have to please him.

When he next turned up at the school, Alice was happy to follow him to the cab, bouncing onto the seat. "Frank, can I have a kitten. Will you get one for me? Mam said I can't have one but she won't say anything if you get one for me. Will you, Frank, will you?"

"I don't know, Alice. If mam has said no…" He didn't get a chance to finish.

"She won't say anything if you bring it home, Frank. Bella said they can go to new homes soon then it will be too late. Please, Frank," Alice pleaded.

"I'm not promising anything, mind, but we'll see. That's all I'll say on the matter. Now, my boss wants to see you again so if you are nice to him, I'll see what I can do. Will you do that, Alice?"

"I will if you get me the kitten," she said cheekily.

Frank smiled but said no more as they entered the driveway of his boss's house.

Alice was shown into the same room as before but she had a little more confidence about her this time, taking a seat on the small sofa when it was offered. The curtains were still drawn to keep out the light but it didn't seem so frightening today. She was happy to talk to the man as he plied her with milk and biscuits this time. He asked her about school, her friends and what she liked doing best so Alice told him about the kittens.

"Well, I'm sure we could find you a kitten. Perhaps if you could come again on a Saturday, you could choose one for yourself. Would you like that?" he asked her.

"Oh yes, that would be lovely but I don't know what my mam would say. She don't want a cat," Alice replied.

"Leave that to Frank. I'm sure he can get your mother to agree. Will you come again, Alice? May I call you Alice?" the man asked.

Alice said he could and giggled a little, thinking he was quite a nice man when you got to know him. She felt sorry for him because he always seemed to be sitting in a gloomy room on his own. This time she took the apples happily as she said goodbye.

It was weeks before she saw Frank outside the school gates again. She thought he had forgotten about the promise but he spoke to her briefly. "I'll pick you up on Saturday close to the school gates at four o'clock. Don't tell anyone where you are going," he said fiercely.

"No, I won't. Will I be picking my kitten?" Alice said, before heading off to catch up with her friends without waiting for a reply.

She had hardly got through the back door before she shouted, "Mam, Mary said the baby chicks will be born on Saturday. Can I go and see them, can I?" Alice found she was quite good at lying.

"Yes alright, stop mithering. It's all you've talked about and it will keep you from under my feet," Mrs Stainbank stated.

Alice was desperate to brag to her friends about the cab ride and the great big house but they wouldn't believe her if she told them. She thought she might be able to bring something back with her, not to steal, just something to show she had been in the grand house. Her secret was threatening to overwhelm her but she knew she would have to keep it just that, a secret. Tomorrow she was going to the house to pick a kitten. She didn't know how she would sleep such was her excitement.

Thankfully Saturday came and Alice spent most of the day playing with her friends, waiting until she could get away. Walking quickly in the opposite direction to her home, she saw the horse and cab, the driver standing by the horse's head waiting for her. She was out of sight as he helped her into the carriage. "Where's Frank?" she asked but the door was closed none too gently behind her and she was alone.

Spreading herself out on the seat, she felt the soft leather with her hands as the horse set off. The upholstery had a lovely smell to it and was an unusual shade of green. She had to stop herself moving the curtain and waving out of the window. She felt nervous without Frank but it was a different feeling to how she felt when he was around.

All too soon, the house loomed and she was helped down. It was dark stone, the stucco crumbling in places though the building was large and foreboding. That was the word… foreboding, Alice said to no one but herself.

"Go up the steps and in through the door. Good luck, lass, you'll need it," the driver told her.

This time Alice wasn't shown into the gloomy room but followed the butler up the broad staircase where, on the landing, large pictures of stern looking men looked down on her. The landing turned at right angles to show another flight of stairs. Alice struggled to keep pace with the man but he stood at the top, waiting for her to catch up. The balcony overlooked the hallway below and a huge chandelier hung from the ceiling, giving off small rainbows of colour where it caught the light. She looked along the corridor. Either side was a mirror image of the other, numerous doors leading to numerous rooms. The butler didn't speak as he strode down to a door at the end which he opened, ushering her inside.

Alice thought the room had the same gloomy feel with the only light coming through a gap in the curtains and a few lamps sitting on cabinets either side of a huge bed. Again, she saw smoke rising from a chair which was behind a large escritoire before her eyes focused on the man sitting there.

"Hello, my dear," the voice said hoarsely.

Alice worried about being in this gentleman's bedroom, feeling very afraid as her voice quavered in her throat. "Hello." She was going to be in big trouble if her dad found out about this.

"Come and sit down next to me," the man told her, patting the chair next to him. "I've a glass of milk for you. I'm sure you would like that, wouldn't you?"

Alice didn't reply but walked slowly toward him and the chair. She knew she shouldn't but somehow couldn't stop her legs from propelling her forward. Taking the glass from his hand, their fingers touched and he tried to stifle a cough. She sipped at the creamy milk but it tasted funny and she grimaced when it hit the back of her throat. It felt warm as it went down into her stomach so she tried a little more, then more until the glass was empty. The man didn't speak but sat watching her, drawing heavily on his cigar.

Alice sat back in the chair. She felt as though she wanted to go to sleep but that would have been rude so she tried to rouse herself.

"I think I'd bedder go." Her words slurred as she attempted to rise from the chair. Her legs wouldn't carry her. She wanted to collapse onto the floor and sleep. Something was wrong. She had never felt like this before, smiling though she didn't know why.

"Let me help you, my dear," the man said as he lifted her into his arms, carrying her to the bed. She wanted to sit up, put her feet onto the floor but she couldn't move. Her head didn't feel right, her body heavy and she felt she was going to be sick. Alice heard the key turn in the door lock before the nightmare began.

She tried screaming. She tried getting off the bed but he pulled her back. She screamed as his hands grabbed at her flesh but no sound came out. He was hurting her, tearing the bodice of her dress. She was going to be in so much trouble. Alice tried to kick, punch, bite but her limbs wouldn't move. It was if her mind and body were separate. She prayed for Frank to come and find her, her mam or dad, anyone. Her mind knew she shouldn't be here. She should tell him to stop but the words wouldn't come out. The pain came out from the top of her head as he forced himself into her and that was the last thing she remembered before passing out completely.

CHAPTER 13

Frank wanted to ensure he had an alibi so he walked into the house, tipping some of his money onto the table without acknowledging his mam or Rachel.

"Will you be in for tea?" Peggy Stainbank asked without turning from the cooker.

"Aye, if that's okay," Frank replied, tapping his fingers on the table, much to the annoyance of the two women. He hated his family and knew from a young age that the feeling was mutual. Everyone gave him a wide berth which suited him fine. He didn't want people to know his business nor that of his boss. As the hands on the clock reached six, Peggy Stainbank took Frank out of his thoughts.

"Nip along to Mary's and get our Alice, will you? Your dad and John will be in any minute."

Frank scraped back his chair and headed for the yard door. Peggy Stainbank had expected some backchat but he had hardly said a word since coming in. She knew she should love all her children equally but her firstborn was hard to like, never mind love.

They all came in through the door at the same time but it

was Frank who spoke first. "Our Alice isn't at Mary's. They said she had never been there and certainly not today."

"Where's that little madam got to? I'll skin her alive, the scheming little minx," Peggy Stainbank said. "I've a good mind to let her go hungry. Come on, everyone sit down and I'll put dinner on the table."

John and Mr Stainbank scrubbed their hands before the latter picked up the bread knife and started slicing the loaf which was sitting on a board next to his plate.

Frank's nerves jangled at every noise, the clattering of the pans, the banging of the oven door, but he knew Alice wouldn't be back yet and he just had to bide his time. The others talked about this and that but he didn't join in with the conversation and no one spoke directly to him. It suited him fine because he really didn't know what he could say.

Once the evening meal was over and there was still no sign of Alice, they became worried. She liked her food did Alice and no one could remember her missing a meal.

"Frank, pop over to our Kate's to see if the little madam has gone there, will you?" his mother said, looking directly at her son for the first time today.

"Why can't he go?" he said, pointing to John.

"Because he's been to work, that's why," she said.

"Well, so have I. Don't I put money into this family? What do you think I do every day?" Frank replied.

No one answered him. "It's alright. I'll go," John said, picking up his coat off the nail on the back of the door. Going out along the back arches, he took a short cut to King Street where he walked along the side of the cemetery to the row of houses on the other side. Kate had moved after her marriage to Ted Williams and was living in what was really her mother-in-law's house because she was there first. John carried on to the lane behind the houses. The yard door would be unlocked and he slipped in before knocking on the back door. He didn't wait for an answer as he stepped inside into the kitchen which was almost the same as the one at home except the stairs didn't start in there and it was always tidy.

Kate stood to greet him. He loved this house. It was always so welcoming, not like his own. His mother tried her best, bless her, but there was always an atmosphere. Looking round, John said, "Oh, I thought Alice might be here. We haven't seen her since this morning. Mam said she's been out all day."

"She hasn't been here. I haven't seen anything of her since last weekend," Kate replied.

John told them the tale that Alice had given about going to see the chickens at Mary's but she had never been there. Ted offered to walk back to see if she had now arrived home or Kate would spend the night worrying.

When they got back to the Stainbank house, they found there had still been no sign of Alice and it was now getting late. She had never been this late before. Mr Stainbank, Frank, John and Ted began knocking on doors to see if anyone else was missing or if they could shed any light on where Alice might be. When they returned with no information, Frank knew he would have to do something before the police were called.

"Let's split up," he said, "and have a quick look further afield and come back in half an hour. If we still haven't found her, I'll go up to Bink Street station myself." The others nodded in agreement. "Dad, you have a look round the pottery and back area. John, can you have a look around the school grounds? Ted, can you look around the back yards, checking on any open doors and I'll go up the road toward the cemetery myself." He was relieved when they all agreed, going out together. He knew where she would be and although he walked quickly when the others were watching,

111

he slowed as he strode out of sight. He had to be the one to find her in case his baby sister said anything. He needed to remind her it was still their secret.

He heard Alice groaning before he saw her propped haphazardly against a gravestone, her dress torn, her hair falling loosely over her face. At first, he couldn't bear to touch her. The bile rose in his throat as he lost his tea in the bushes. What had he done? He had provided girls before but he didn't know them, they meant nothing to him. He had never seen or felt their pain. His boss was becoming more choosy, those from the slums were not good enough anymore. What on earth had he done? No one would be on his side now but his priority was to get Alice to safety.

Picking her up in his arms, her head lolled back, a gurgling in her throat.

"Don't try to speak, Alice. You'll be safe now." Frank made the decision to take her to Kate's because her house was nearer and he couldn't yet face the rest of his family. He needed time to get his story straight in his mind. He would need to make sure Alice didn't say anything about their secret, and he would have to make out he didn't know what had happened when he spoke to her.

The front door was nearer and he kicked it hard as he continued to talk to Alice. Kate screamed when she saw them, opening the door wide and ushering them in.

"Lay her on the sofa," Kate shouted, grabbing a blanket off the back to put over Alice. "Where was she? What's happened to her?"

Frank shook his head as he looked at his hand which was smeared in blood, glad his stomach was empty otherwise he would have made a fool of himself. "Can I leave her with you? I need to let the others know I've found her and I'll get the doctor on my way to work." Frank wanted to escape as quickly as possible. Running home, he was in a cold sweat, wishing he had never agreed to let Alice go to the house.

Deep down he knew what would happen but he thought she might cry for a few days and then it would be forgotten. If this got out, he would be in big trouble for procuring girls. His boss had enough money to buy his own way out of any trouble. But not Frank. This would be the last time, time to move on, but that would be easier said than done. What had possessed him to use Alice? He knew the answer. His boss was getting choosy. Frank had a reputation and the only people who would employ him would be other thugs. What kind of a mess had he got himself in? He would have to make sure Alice didn't say anything, that was his priority.

He flopped in the chair, explaining only that it looked like Alice had been attacked and he would go for the doctor on his way to work. Kate would look after her until then. Peggy Stainbank wanted to go straight round to see her baby but Frank suggested it might not be safe and to wait for Ted to walk with her. He wanted to get out of the house before the others returned, making the excuse that he would need to catch the doctor.

IT WAS several hours before the doctor arrived and John and Rachel had returned home as there really wasn't enough room for them all in the small living room. Mr and Mrs Stainbank wanted to stay and speak to him about what had happened.

The doctor gave Alice laudanum so she would sleep before taking Kate and Mrs Stainbank to one side. "Your sister has been attacked and raped, I'm afraid. I have given her something which for the short time will ease her pain. Can you get her into a bed where it's quiet? Yes, that's what she needs, quiet."

The women held on to each other, taking in the doctor's words, unable to understand why this had happened.

Peggy Stainbank went to her youngest child, sitting

stroking her daughter's hand before covering her face. She broke down in great sobbing tears. The poor child, for this to happen to her. She jerked when the doctor spoke again.

"I'm afraid I am going to have to report this to the police but I will explain she won't be up to making a statement until tomorrow. Goodnight, Mrs Williams. I'll call again tomorrow so I can write my report for the police. Goodnight Mr Stainbank, Mrs Stainbank."

AFTER SHE HAD SHOWN the doctor out, Kate put her arms round her mam and cried until there were no tears left. Mr Stainbank and Ted talked uncomfortably with Mrs Williams in the kitchen, not really knowing what to say. In the end, Mr Stainbank returned home before his temper got the better of him. He wanted to strike out at someone, anyone. He left his wife to sit with Alice, saying he would call in early in the morning, when they might learn a little more about what had happened.

Both houses were distraught by the day's events and no one got much sleep that night. Peggy Stainbank and Kate sat uncomfortably in chairs in the lounge all night as Alice was drugged into an induced sleep. Each move made the poor girl groan but she did not waken.

Over the next few days, people came and went, including the police but they were turned away as Alice continued to sleep. The doctor had noted bruises on her wrists, forearms and inner thighs. After three days, he decided to reduce the laudanum to allow her to awake gradually. He explained to Kate and Mrs Stainbank that the physical wounds would heal but he was worried about her mental state as she awoke. As soon as she came round, they were to give her as much tepid water as she could manage, then bread soaked in warm milk with a drop of brandy to take the edge off. They were to let him know when she was awake and he would liaise with the police so they could get a statement.

It was almost two weeks since the attack before they managed to give Alice any food though she had to be encouraged like a baby to take anything. The first time Kate had tried to give her the bread and milk with brandy, Alice became upset, pushing the spoon away. Her eyes, which had seemed dead, suddenly grew large as she shrank back into the pillows as though she was being poisoned.

Alice hadn't uttered a word only groaned when Mrs Stainbank tried to wash her gently. Her hair was still matted and she refused to have it brushed. Both women were worried. They tried to talk to her but she didn't respond. When she was awake, she looked up to the ceiling, not moving even as people came in and out of the room.

The police had called to ask her questions but she stared blankly past them. There had been no more attacks but they couldn't find anyone who knew where Alice had been or who with. All they could do was continue with patrols in the area and monitor the school gates for anyone suspicious. If she began talking, they were to be informed as any information would be helpful, they said.

The bruising on her body had turned from black to purple to yellow as the physical scars began to fade but Alice still didn't utter a word. She either lay with her eyes closed, feigning sleep or staring blankly at the ceiling, and no amount of coaxing could get her to respond.

CHAPTER 14

Mr Stainbank couldn't bear to see his daughter in this state so it was John who made the daily trips to see her after work. For some reason, Alice was more relaxed when John sat on the edge of the bed in the cramped room, talking to her about his day. The involuntary flexing of her fingers and hand grabbing of the blankets stopped, though the blank stare remained.

He never seemed to find it a problem giving his monologue each day, telling her how they all missed her. It was as he was saying that she would soon be home and in her own bed that the screaming and thrashing began. It took both Kate and Mrs Stainbank to hold her down while John went for the doctor.

When he finally arrived, Alice had gone back to sleep, her ague released. It was a good sign the doctor explained, the floodgates were now open and while it was disturbing, it would eventually abate. He gave Kate a mild sedative to give her if and when required but said there was little more he could do. Love and time was all that was necessary now and she was getting plenty of both.

Alice refused to get up out of the bed even for a wash,

pulling the blankets around her like a cocoon until they were at their wits end as to what to do. Kate carried water up and down the stairs and the same with the pot but knew it couldn't go on. Everyone talked at her but whatever the conversation, she gave no response.

When they finally got her up out of bed to sit in a chair, Alice was sick which they put down to her lingering in bed for too long.

Each morning Kate encouraged her to get up but she continued to be sick, retching into the pot even though she had hardly eaten anything. It was Mrs Williams who hit the nail on the head. The lass was pregnant, there was no denying it, she told Kate. The doctor was called again but he said it was too early to give a prognosis but it was a possibility.

John, to try and be useful, called in at the police station to tell them how Alice was getting on and to see if they were any further forward in finding the culprit. Although they had no further information, they believed it was a one off but were continuing with their enquiries. What they needed was Alice to talk to them as she was the only one who could shed any light on who her attacker was, and where the attack took place because there was no evidence it had happened in the cemetery where she was found. They needed to know where she was before and more importantly, who with.

John was repeating the conversation to the family when Frank came in at the tail end of the conversation.

"I thought they must have dropped the case?" he said, looking at John.

"Oh no, they are hoping Alice will at least explain where she was on the nights she said she was at Mary's. They think they are linked. Don't forget she had been lying for weeks about where she had been so perhaps she had been meeting someone," John said to no one in particular.

"You sound like the police yourself. What do you know about it?" Frank goaded him.

Jumping to his feet, John grabbed Frank's arm. "I'll tell you what I know about it, I'll kill the bastard who did this to our Alice when I find out who it was."

As they faced up to each other, Mr Stainbank stepped in between them. "Stop it, the both of you. There's been enough trouble brought to this household without you two being at each other's throats."

John stood his ground as Frank pulled his arm away.

"You haven't got the bottle," Frank snarled, marching back the way he came.

The uneasiness in both households continued but outwardly Alice looked to be getting better, apart from her eyes which had lost their sparkle. Any life in her seemed to have been taken away. She would at least get up, dressed and sit with Kate and Mrs Williams while watching young Edward play but she never started a conversation or contributed much other than monosyllables. John continued to visit and that made her brighten slightly. Kate worried what would happen to the girl once the baby was born. The house wasn't big enough to house them all and Ted had been patience itself, saying Alice would return home in her own time, though the same couldn't be said for Mrs Williams who was of the opinion that Alice was being pandered to.

Days went into weeks, weeks into months where Alice had never set foot outside the front door. The weather had been atrocious for days, snow a foot deep, the temperature never rising above freezing all day. Peggy Stainbank and John had been full of cold so stayed away. Only Ted came home each day with news from the outside world.

At first the three women got on each other's nerves, Alice saying nothing, Mrs Williams talking incessantly while Kate tried to be peacemaker. She had tried to encourage Alice to read but the book sat unopened in her lap.

It was five months before Alice spoke about her ordeal and this was brought about by two events on the same day. Kate was upstairs with Edward when the coal man arrived with much needed coal. The yard door had swollen with the wet weather so she called to Alice to go into the yard and open the door for him. As she forced the door open, before turning away, Alice saw the horse and cart. The sight of it made her hyperventilate in the cold air, forcing her to almost choke. This turned into a fit of coughing and as she struggled to breath, she was on the verge of her legs giving way.

The coal man emptied the coal sack into the coalhouse next to the lav before attempting to take Alice by the arm to help her inside. The sound of her screaming brought Kate and Mrs Williams to the back door to see what the fuss was all about.

"I don't know what happened, Mrs!" the coal man said to the two women. "She's almost collapsed as she opened the door."

Kate took Alice by the hand, turning to take her into the house. "I'm sorry, Mr, she's had a bad time. It's not you."

"Aye, I heard and I'm real sorry for the lass," he replied. "She always liked to pat the horse and now she's petrified."

After paying the coal man and forcing the gate shut, Kate returned to the house where Alice was sitting in the chair, shaking, while Mrs Williams tried to console her by patting her gently on her arm.

"Come on, Alice, stop it now. You'll make yourself ill." Kate had almost lost patience with the girl. "Come on, have some water, stop shaking, take deep breaths, come on now."

Later in the day, Kate was preparing the evening meal in the kitchen while Mrs Williams was attempting to show Alice how to crochet a shawl for the baby when there was a knock on the front door. Alice remained in her seat while Mrs Williams struggled to get up to answer it.

It was Frank, reluctantly coming in from the freezing

cold. Alice took one look at him, and let out an ear piercing scream before rushing at him, scratching his face before he managed to grab her hands.

"What on earth is going on?" Kate said, coming in from the kitchen, wiping her hands on her apron. "Hello, Frank. What can we do for you?"

"I was hoping for a cup of tea to warm me up but I see I'm not welcome, by her anyway. I've just come to let you know mam's took really bad. The doctor thinks it's pneumonia. Rachel's doing her best but we are out all day. If you could pop over, we'd be grateful."

"You can see how I'm fixed, Frank, so I'll make no promises but I'll see what I can do. If I don't manage to get over in the next few days, will you let me know how she is?"

"No, no, no, not him. Don't let him come here," Alice screamed. "I never want to see him again. Get him out, get out and leave me alone," she yelled, trying to grab Frank, to punch him, to kick him as though possessed.

"I'll leave you to it, Kate. I think she's gone mad." He glanced at Alice. "Mam would be pleased to see you though if you can. Tarrah then." He was glad to get out into the cold air. He'd have to watch himself, perhaps if he could get the others to see Alice had gone mad, he might just get himself out of trouble. What a mess. He shook his head and the snow which had settled on his cap fell to his shoulders.

BACK AT KATE'S they were getting no sense out of Alice. She was rocking backward and forward, her hands clutching at her dress while mumbling loudly, incoherently. No amount of cajoling or hugging would stop her and in the end Kate slapped her hard across her face.

"Stop it, Alice. You'll make yourself ill. Either tell me what's upset you or forget it. Now come on."

The shock of the slap stopped Alice temporarily so she

jumped from the chair, shouting, "You know nowt, our Kate. You don't know what it's like for me having to keep a secret. I can't stand it anymore." Alice began to cry softly as her temper abated.

"What secret? What secret, Alice? Come on now, you can tell me anything you know that? Has it got anything to do with our Frank?" Kate took the girl's hands in case she lashed out at her. "You might as well tell me or I'll go and ask Frank myself. I will. Come on, now."

Alice nodded as Kate and Mrs Williams looked at each other before she spoke again. "It was our secret. I wasn't to tell no one. He promised me a kitten but he lied, he always lies."

"What happened, Alice? Why did you and Frank have a secret? Listen to me. No one is going to hurt you now so you might as well tell me."

Alice cried and cried, snot running down her nose, sobbing uncontrollably, her head resting on Kate's shoulder. She hoped Alice would finally talk but instead she almost went into a faint so she had no choice but to help her to lay on the sofa. The girl lay quietly, her head turned away from them to try to hide the tears falling through her lashes. Not wanting to say any more, she closed her eyes until she fell into a fitful sleep.

Kate picked up Edward before following Mrs Williams into the kitchen where they talked in hushed voices while the boy played on the floor.

"You'll need to tell the police," Mrs Williams said.

"Tell them what? That my sister has almost lost her mind and we don't know what she is telling us. I can't do that, I can't accuse my brother. What am I accusing him of? No, I'll have to try to speak to her again to see if I can get some more information. Now let's say no more about it." But for Kate, the matter was far from closed. She would have to speak to her husband about it before talking to dad or John. The family had gone through enough without her accusing one of their own.

She waited until they were laid side by side in bed before Kate told Ted what had occurred with Frank. He agreed with Kate that they couldn't go in mob handed to accuse Frank without some evidence and when and if they did, the police were the best people to deal with it. She would have to try and coax more out of Alice first before going to her father with information. He didn't like her keeping things from her family but in this instance it would be better to get all the facts before everyone started fighting amongst themselves. Frank had obviously disturbed Alice, though she was in a bit of a state before he arrived at the house so he may have nothing to do with what had happened. They both nodded their heads, knowing that in reality Frank could know more than he was letting on.

CHAPTER 15

There was a sudden thaw in the weather but everyone was still giving each other the cold shoulder in the Williams household. By early afternoon, a weak sun had water running in channels where the cart wheels had been. Putting on her boots, coat, scarf and mittens, Kate wrapped her shawl around her head and shoulders to visit the Stainbank household. She didn't really like leaving her mother-in-law with both her son and Alice but she needed to know how mam was and more importantly needed a break from the house. By the time she had slipped and side-stepped puddles and snow, she was nithered as she opened the back door of her old home. She shouted a welcome, took off her outer clothes, and put the kettle on before opening the door into the living room.

Peggy Stainbank had lain on the sofa for the past few weeks in an effort to keep warm but the fire was now getting low. Her skin looked wan, her eyes tired as she struggled to breathe but she was glad, very glad to see Kate. Beads of perspiration rested on her top lip, her breathing laboured when she tried to speak.

"Eh, lass, I'm so glad to see you. I'm bored to death, laying here day after day like a lazy old goat." She laughed which sent her into a frenzy of coughing before groaning with pain. Her head fell back onto the pillow while she tried to get her shallow breathing under control.

"Are you feeling any better, mam? Could you manage to sit up and have a cup of tea? I've brought a pie for you all as I don't suppose Rachel has much time to cook. It will just need warming in the oven." Kate put her arm under her mother to help her sit up. She could feel how thin she had become.

"One question at a time, lass," she said. Her chest rattled with each intake of breath. "I'm feeling a little better but am so cold even in here with the blankets over me. I've got extra clothes on and I'm still cold. Look, the fires almost out and I don't have the energy to get up and put coal on it," she gasped.

"I'll brew the tea and get some more coal for the fire," Kate answered, getting up from the sofa.

They sat, mother and daughter, one not asking the questions the other one did not want to give answers to so they talked generally about anything. In the end it was Peggy Stainbank who asked the question. "How's Alice? I miss her. She would be good company for me."

Kate wasn't sure what to say but thought her mother deserved to know what happened the day Frank called round. She explained how Alice had become hysterical. The screaming had become nerve shredding as she shouted more incoherently. "What do you think?" Kate asked.

"Well, if our Frank had something to do with it then it could be anything," she replied slowly, almost in a whisper. "He's always been shifty that one but not that, no not that. I can't believe he would stoop so low, not even him surely, his own sister. We don't know what he does to earn his money but not that, lass, not that."

"I don't know what to think," Kate said. "I need to try and coax more out of her before we go to the police. Ted agrees we shouldn't confront Frank until we know the truth so please don't say anything, not yet."

"I can't mention it to your dad or John or they'll do for him and where would that leave us?" Peggy said as Kate was getting into her outdoor clothing. Peggy Stainbank had been so pleased to see her eldest daughter but the news had left her exhausted to the bone.

"Don't say anything to Frank either. We don't want him to get wind of this if he is involved. Let's wait and see what transpires. I'll call again as soon as I can if the weather holds." Kate gave her a hug which made the woman cough again.

WHEN KATE RETURNED HOME, it was to find Mrs Williams in the kitchen, peeling vegetables while Alice seemed to have remained in the same position as when she had left. Edward was fortunately asleep in his pram.

"How is she, lass?" Mrs Williams asked as she wiped her hands, putting a cup out for Kate to get some tea which was always brewing in the large brown teapot.

"Not good, she needs someone there during the day to make sure she's warm and has plenty of hot drinks. Rachel's doing the best she can but you know none of them get home before six." Kate looked toward Alice who didn't even acknowledge her presence.

Leaving Mrs Williams in the kitchen, Kate stood in front of Alice. "Right, miss, you've sat here wallowing long enough. What's done is done and you'll have to live with it. Tomorrow we are going over home to air off your bed and you can make yourself useful looking after mam. Do you hear me, Alice?"

"I'll not go back there, Kate. I'll kill myself first. Do you hear me, I'll not go back to that house while he's there. I won't and you can't make me." Alice's voice was getting louder.

"Well, you'd better start talking, my girl, or I'll put you out myself. This can't go on any longer. Mam needs help, and you are the only one who can. Why won't you go home and don't tell me it's a secret 'cause I'll have no more of it. Spit it out, girl, come on. What has all this to do with Frank?"

Alice stood to try and leave the room but Kate stood in front of her to stop her.

"Sit down, Alice. This is my house and we welcomed you here but mam needs you so you'll have to get on with it. What or who are you frightened of?" Kate pushed her back onto the seat. "All those days you were late home from school, where did you go? If you don't tell me what went on, I'll get the police back and they can interview you at the police station."

Alice took a deep breath. "I went for a ride in a cab. It was nice at first…" She struggled to get her words out.

"Whose cab? Who took you in that cab, Alice?" Kate tried to say it softly so the child would not close up.

"Our Frank. He used to meet me from school sometimes and give me things, ribbons, money. He said I could go to his boss's house for a look round and feed the horse. They promised to get me a kitten and I so wanted a kitten," she sobbed.

"Then what happened?" Kate looked at her youngest sister, feeling more sorry for her by the minute.

"This, this is what happened." Alice pulled at her stomach. "I didn't want to do it, I just wanted to look round the house. He gave me a drink of milk which tasted funny then I felt dizzy. I won't tell you any more," she cried. "I can't tell you any more 'cause I don't know."

"There, there, Alice, I promise you it will be alright. Now you've got to tell the police what you told me. Can you do that, Alice? I know, I know it's upsetting for you but they have to know." Kate took the girl's hands in hers.

Alice just nodded. "What about Frank?"

"Let the police sort him out. You're a very brave girl. Now, come on, stop crying. It's over." Kate hugged her tightly. "He won't hurt you now, I'll make sure of that."

When Alice retired for the night, Kate talked to Ted about the new information and he promised to call into the police station on his way to work the following day though no one knew what would happen to Frank. What they did agree on was that no one should mention it to him. It was better not to get involved nor to give him the chance to abscond. Let the police take whatever action they thought necessary and hope to catch the perpetrator, though obviously Frank was heavily involved which didn't look good.

Kate desperately wanted to go and see her mam to see how she was but couldn't leave Alice alone as she didn't know what time the police would arrive. Yes, Mrs Williams was there but she wasn't Alice's family and to be fair she had her hands full looking after Edward since Alice had moved in, though he was a happy, placid child just like his father.

The girl jumped each time someone walked past the window but it was just people attempting to go about their business while the sleet didn't settle on the ground. Although the snow had finally melted, it was still bitterly cold so the houses had kept their coal fires burning, giving a thin smog outside which swirled and turned like dervishes as people rushed through it.

It was almost two o'clock before the constable arrived. He took off his cap giving it a shake while wiping his feet on the clippie mat by the door. Kate took his hat from him, along with his cape before ushering him inside to the warmth of the room. Alice sat in her usual pose, just staring, plucking at her dress with her fingers. Mrs Williams brought in a kitchen chair for the constable to sit on, opposite the sofa where Kate sat herself next to Alice, gripping her hands.

The only words the constable said to Alice was to take her time and to start at the beginning. He took copious notes, turning pages on his small notebook quickly as the child, and she was still a child, talked quietly. It was like a relief valve opening. It was no longer a secret she had to deal with on her own. It had apparently started months before the attack when Frank would meet her from school where it seemed he had coerced her into getting into the cab, taking her to his boss's house.

Kate was amazed that they had never picked up on Frank's connection before though he always ensured he never returned to the house at the same time as Alice. He had always been vague about his whereabouts at any time, even before they moved to Middlesbrough.

When Alice finished talking, she took a deep breath. At the same time, there was a tap on the door and Mrs Williams came in with a tray of tea and griddle scones. Kate knew she would have been listening at the door but the whole neighbourhood would know the family's plight soon enough. Alice sat back with her eyes closed, her grey skin no longer drawn like an old woman. She was still extremely pale as Kate looked at her but finally it seemed her baby sister had found some peace.

The constable had been in the house almost two hours before he stood to take his leave, saying they would arrest Frank as soon as possible to help with their enquiries. He was sorry for the family's woes but hoped the girl, as he called Alice, would be able to rebuild her life in some way. It was a sad day for all concerned.

After seeing the policeman out, Kate picked up her coat and shawl before saying she needed to slip along to see her mother.

"Aye lass, get yerself away," Mrs Williams said but they were both shocked when Alice said she wanted to see her as well.

The two of them hurried through the streets, heads down against the rain which now seemed relentless. Alice was leaning heavily on Kate's arm as she was still very weak. As they turned into the bottom of the street, they didn't see the figure on the opposite side of the road change direction, going back the way he had come.

Peggy Stainbank was delighted to see Alice. The child was still her baby and she missed her terribly especially while she had been ill. They hugged and cried until she began gasping for breath. Kate rushed to get her a cup of water. Her words were rasping and they couldn't really understand what she was saying. Eventually she lay back on the pillow, tears running down her face, but this time they were happy tears.

While Alice was sent to the kitchen to make a pot of tea, Kate brought her up to date with what had happened and the fact that the police would now be looking for Frank.

"Eh, that lad's always had the devil in him but to do this… well, he's insane. I just can't believe he'd do something so terrible to our Alice. Surely the child has got it wrong." Mrs Stainbank saw Kate shake her head. "Well, I'm done with him. He's no child of mine." It came out in gasps.

Kate stressed to her not to say anything to Frank if she saw him before the police caught up with him as they didn't know what he would do. They would have to get back to see to Edward's tea. Mrs Williams had been a godsend, she said, but the woman couldn't manage everything.

As they set off home, Kate linked Alice's arm and for the first time in months both had smiles on their faces as they walked slowly home. The visit seemed to have perked Alice up, not just seeing her mam but unburdening herself to the policeman.

CHAPTER 16

Peggy Stainbank heard the voices as the men hurried in through the back door. Before she could tell them what had transpired, John told her there had been a big fight outside the public house in the village. He didn't know what it was about but men were throwing punches left, right and centre, so he had skirted round behind the buildings.

She said she also had some news. Kate and Alice had been over after talking to the police about Frank. The men were shocked to hear what had happened. John put on his coat and cap, saying he had to go back out. Mr Stainbank didn't see him pick up the bread knife which was on the kitchen table but his mam did. She tried to shout to stop her son doing something stupid but the sharp intake of breath made her cough. She knew what John would do to Frank and hoped, prayed, her youngest boy would be safe.

John walked the streets, looking for his brother, but only mad dogs would be out on a night like this. The village was unduly quiet after the melee earlier in the evening. For the first time in his life, he walked into the public bar of the Cleveland Hotel and asked for a double whisky, putting his money on the counter. He looked around for his brother but there was no sign of him. The barman confirmed he hadn't seen him but that wasn't unusual in itself. John said his mother had taken a turn for the worse and he needed to let his brother know. A wizened old man in the corner playing dominoes with an equally decrepit man said he might be found near St Barnabas Church doing business. John finished his drink, shuddered and wondered what men and women saw in it, said goodnight and wandered back into the gloom.

The incessant rain muted any other noises as John tried to keep his senses alert to anyone close by. Surely only a madman would be doing business outside on a night like this. But then his brother was mad, there was little doubt about that. There was no one about as he crept around the outside of the church building and although he was beginning to shiver with the cold, the glow of the whisky in his stomach, and the feel of the knife in the inside pocket of his coat drove him on. He was still keeping to the shadows of the trees when he saw a cab stop on the road opposite and Frank jump out. The only noise apart from the rain was the slamming of the door before the horse and cab moved on.

John waited, watching Frank who crossed the road quickly heading toward home. John tried to quicken his pace. The last place he wanted to confront his brother was at home but he didn't want to get too close and be seen until he was ready. Stopping under a large oak tree, he moved the knife up the sleeve of his right arm but this allowed Frank to get a good way ahead so he had to think quickly. Crossing the road, he entered the back arch where he ran, side-stepping the rubbish and on to the opening at the other end. Picking up a stone, John continued on the opposite side of the road. A little way ahead was the cutting to the beck where he had played as a child. He hadn't been there for years but thought it would be a good place to lure Frank.

Throwing the stone with his left hand, he crouched into a doorway, watching as Frank stopped when it hit his shoulder. John watched him look round and he thought he was going to carry on but he crossed the road and went into the gap. Not quite running, he didn't want to be out of breath, John walked quickly, taking the knife from his sleeve, holding it tightly in his right hand which he put behind his back.

As he reached the cutting, Frank was on his way out but John blocked his exit. Although John was almost four years younger and as thin as a bean pole, he stood a good six inches taller than his brother. Frank had the advantage of being much stockier but also much more worldly wise in the art of holding his own in a fight.

The torrential rain stopped suddenly, the silence like an audience waiting for the play to begin. The watery moon shone weakly on the two principal players. Both stood facing each other, waiting for their cue to begin.

"Ah, little brother. What?" Frank said, smirking, but stepped back when he saw the knife in John's hand.

The knife sliced at his arm and he laughed but John was now filled with such anger and rage at the thought of Alice that he plunged the knife toward Frank's stomach, jabbing manically at his brother through his clothing. It was ineffective against the heavy coat Frank was wearing. He lunged again with more force, managing to unseat the single button which bounced onto the wet pavement before rolling away.

The only sound as they moved apart was the heavy breathing of both men combined with water dripping intermittently onto a tin roof. Both took another step backwards as if to take in what was happening. John knew his life wouldn't be worth living if he didn't finish what he set out to do. As Frank took a step forward, he rushed at him, jabbing as hard as he could. The bread knife wasn't the best choice, he needed to push in and out, slice, push, slice but his wrist was grabbed as was his shoulder.

"Haven't got the bottle, that's what you said." John spoke through gritted teeth, spittle landing on his chin.

"You can't do it, little brother. You can't finish me off," Frank growled, realising he was bleeding and looking down before looking John in the eye.

John head butted him. The bone cracked and Frank's nose began bleeding as he released his grip. John pushed the knife in as far as he could. The brothers were so close they could almost be hugging. John knew he would lose this fight and he would be a dead man if Frank got hold of the knife. Twisting the knife, he pushed once more. Frank's hand reached to his stomach, making a strange groan while trying to move backwards and grab the knife at the same time. Pulling it back, John sliced at his brother's fingers, both momentarily looking at the blood pouring over the now bright red shirt.

John took in a deep breath to get some air into his lungs, moving back to get some space between them. He watched Frank trying to hold his intestines in place. Neither spoke but their eyes locked before Frank staggered forward, falling flat on his face, blood running from both his head and stomach.

John was about to fling the knife into the bushes but thought better of it. It could incriminate him and he wasn't sure if Frank was really dead. He plucked up the courage to kick him. His brother didn't move but he kept his eyes on him as he stepped backwards out of the cutting.

A pewter cloud covered the moon, ending any light on the scene, and the rain began to bounce up off the pavement as if in applause that the villain had been slain. John didn't feel triumphant, he just wanted the curtain to come down on what had happened.

It seemed as though he had been out for hours but he could only have been standing in the cut for minutes. He needed to get home, to put it behind him, to forget it if he ever could. After all, he had done it for Alice but she must never know or they would both be damned.

By now John was shaking and he wasn't sure whether it was the cold wet weather or what he had done. He held his hands out to the rain to take away the evilness of what had happened. Would he now hang instead of his brother? He felt sick, he had to get away before he was seen.

Wanting to run, but afraid to draw attention to himself should any other idiot be out on a night like this, he walked quickly, as though getting out of the rain and headed off back toward the main road. He turned back on himself and toward the ginnel, into the back arches. He propped his back against the wall and for the first time he could remember, he cried. His shoulders heaved and he went down on his haunches. Head in his hands, he sobbed not only for himself but for Alice, for his mam. What time it was he didn't know but he knew he would have to pull himself together before he got home. The enormity of what he had done hit him in waves but deep down he was glad, glad he had for the first time got one over on his brother so he would never hurt anyone again.

OPENING the door as quietly as he could, John shook off his cap, removing his coat before hanging them on the hook next to his dad's. In the dim light he could see no blood on his hands but washed them and his face somewhat obsessively before drying them on the piece of sacking by the cooker. He cleaned the knife before replacing it on the bread board. It seemed such a mundane task but he knew he would never be able to touch it again.

As he opened the door into the living room, he could see the others had already gone to their beds and his mother was sleeping on the sofa. Her face looked peaceful. He looked at her in the shadow of the embers of the fire. He tried to sidestep past her quietly but she opened her eyes.

"John, what have you done? I saw you take the knife," she wheezed.

"I'm sorry, mam, but I had to do it for our Alice," he sobbed as she held out her hand.

"Frank has a dark soul. No, that's not right, he has no soul. He is evil, something is missing from his conscience that's for sure. I wish for God's sake you hadn't done it but he would have got out of it somehow. Now what's done is done and we'll never talk about it again. Get out of your wet clothes before you catch your death." The last word hung like a curtain, both trying to block out what had happened.

"Goodnight, mam."

"Goodnight, son, and God keep you safe."

THE INCLEMENT WEATHER had finally abated although it was still very cold but Kate was desperate to find out what had happened to Frank. She, along with her husband and Alice, who was pushing Edward's pram, walked along to the Stainbank's to see if they had any news. She hoped and prayed that her brother had been arrested and would then tell the police what had happened to Alice and by whom.

They were surprised to see Peggy Stainbank sitting up with a blanket over her knees, talking to two police constables. She was wiping her eyes with a handkerchief as she listened to them but they stopped talking when the others arrived. Repeating what they had already told Mrs Stainbank, they said that they believed the body that had been found near the beck was Frank's but they needed someone to identify him. They seemed to think that his demise was to do with the fight which had occurred the previous evening in the village and must have spilt over. They were concerned that they might have more than one attacker because the knives used were different. The one which killed Frank had a serrated edge. They had already arrested several men in connection with the affray and were sure one or more of them would eventually admit to the murder. They were sorry to be the bearer of bad news, and said the body would be in the mortuary until the family could arrange a funeral. Ted offered to go along with the constables to confirm the body was indeed Frank's though it seemed there was little doubt as the constables knew him. Everyone was surprised when the constable asked if anyone had any questions and Alice piped up.

"What will happen to the man in the big house if Frank is dead?"

"If we find enough evidence, we will bring him to trial but you may have to go on the witness stand," the constable said but Alice didn't reply. "We now only have your word unless we can find anyone else. We will of course speak to any of the staff but they won't give much away because they will be afraid to lose their job."

Kate watched Alice as she looked down. She looked so child like, well, she was a child at thirteen. She should have been waiting to go into her final year at school instead she would be a mother before her fourteenth birthday.

Ted walked out with the constables, saying to Kate to wait for his return and she nodded, wanting to ask a million questions of her mother as to what had happened but didn't want to do so in front of the police, or Alice for that matter.

Mrs Stainbank seemed vague as to what had actually happened to Frank, just saying it was the people he mixed with and it was only a matter of time before he got his comeuppance which Kate thought harsh. It might not be him, Kate said, but her mother seemed to have no doubt. He hadn't been seen since yesterday morning and although that wasn't unusual in itself, she had a feeling in the pit of her stomach that the body they had found was her son's. She took her handkerchief to her eyes to wipe her tears but they were for not for her firstborn but for her youngest boy. She worried what would become of John if anyone found out it was him who had killed his brother.

JOHN WAS STRUGGLING with what he had done but knew he had to remain quiet or he would go to the noose for his crime. He was having night sweats and nightmares over what he had done. When he woke in the dark, he could see Frank's bed and he thought he could see the outline of his brother sleeping. It bothered him so much he hardly dared close his eyes, and when he did it was to see the look on his brother's face as he jabbed at him with the knife and this haunted his dreams. He saw Frank with his eyes wide, glaring at him as he plunged the knife into his skin, his tongue hanging grotesquely from his mouth but it was his words, the way he had sneered at him which upset John the most.

He began calling out in his sleep but fortunately no one could hear his words as he lay in his bed in the attic. His nerves were on edge during the day, causing him to stutter. Those close to him thought it was the shock of what had happened to Alice and now Frank. Poor John was a sensitive lad, everyone said.

NO ONE WANTED to go to Frank's funeral, certainly not John or Alice but Peggy Stainbank insisted that they all put on a united front. Mrs Williams offered to remain at the house with Edward, to serve drinks for anyone who came back. Peggy Stainbank was determined that she would go to her son's funeral though she was still very weak, although the pneumonia was slowly getting better. Rachel asked Dr Hylton if she could borrow the bath chair for her mother so she was pushed to the door of the church but she was adamant she would walk in, which she did with the help of her husband and John. Behind them walked Kate with her husband then Rachel holding on to Alice which was unusual in itself as children didn't normally attend funerals, often only the men would attend but Mrs Stainbank wanted them all to stick together. She wanted the family together as there was enough gossip on the streets.

A few of the neighbours attended, those who were not at work, and Mr Roth was also there. Kate was pleased that Frank's boss had kept away as she was sure one or more of them would have attacked him. She didn't know how Alice would have reacted either. The police hadn't been in touch about an arrest but the family didn't know if that was normal.

The service and burial were sombre as expected, nothing much said about Frank and the Stainbanks were glad when it was all over. There were few tears shed for Frank and no money for a headstone. It was as though no one really wanted to mourn him and once he was in the earth he could be forgotten. Mrs Stainbank felt that her son's soul would belong to the devil and no amount of praying and mourning would change that. Her priority was to keep the rest of the family safe, especially Alice and now John. The poor lad had always been thin but he was now a bag of bones, his nerves getting the better of him. She let people think he was like this because of the shock over his elder brother's demise. She could keep the truth a secret, but could he? It was eating him up inside. He would have to learn to live with it if he was going to cope with what he'd done.

Only a few of the men returned to the house for a drink so it wasn't long before the family were clearing plates from the table. Kate was putting her crockery back into Edward's pram to take home. There was enough cold food to take for supper so they said their goodbyes, leaving the gloom of her family with their thoughts.

. . .

THAT WEEKEND there were great changes in both households. Alice decided it was time to go home. Mrs Williams said a silent prayer that her house would be again a place of calm and young Edward could return to his own room. He would now get Alice's bed. Mr Stainbank and John went to Kate's on the Saturday afternoon after work to collect Alice and her belongings which had been folded into bags. The cot was taken to pieces to be taken once Alice's baby was born.

John was pleased to see Frank's bed moved out of the attic room and into the bedroom with Rachel. He hoped he would sleep better on his own.

Peggy Stainbank also returned to her bed upstairs and no one mentioned Frank again. She was so pleased to have Alice home and that seemed to perk her up now she had company every day. The child set to cleaning and scrubbing in an attempt to take the malaise out of the living room, making it homely again. Her belly was growing bigger but she never talked about being pregnant nor the fact that she was petrified to actually give birth.

They saw Kate several times a week as she brought shopping from the market, butcher's, baker's or whatever they required for Alice to cook under her mother's supervision, though she struggled with everything. The girl still wouldn't leave the house and no cajoling or arguing made any difference so they let her be. Progress had been made by her return home and that was enough for now.

On the ninth of April 1888, Alice gave birth to a daughter. Her labour was long and hard as her small frame struggled to cope with childbirth. The doctor was called when the afterbirth wouldn't come away, and there was so much blood they were afraid she would die. After the doctor had stitched Alice up, he turned to Mrs Stainbank and said, "I don't think your daughter will be capable of having any more children,

I'm afraid. Her insides have been ripped and torn, first when she was raped and now with the birth. I'm sorry. I have done the best I can." He took the two half crowns from her hand. "Keep an eye on her. She is very weak."

Alice was slow to regain her strength though she attempted to feed the baby who whined constantly. Rachel complained she was getting no sleep when she needed to be up for work. After three weeks, tempers were becoming frayed. Alice's hormones gave way to crying which made the baby cry even more. The child whom she had named Clara had no father's name on the birth certificate, in essence a bastard. This caused consternation in the household. The child wouldn't be baptised so her soul wouldn't go to heaven. Alice didn't want to attend to her daughter's needs and Mrs Stainbank struggled with the extra work a baby brings.

Kate could see how hard it was for her mam to care for both Alice and the baby as well as trying to do the cooking and cleaning but she also understood why Alice didn't want to bond with the child. How could she when Clara wasn't born out of love like Edward, and Kate knew how hard giving birth was but she had wanted her baby, loving him unconditionally.

PART IV

CHAPTER 17

KATE 1888 MIDDLESBROUGH

Kate had a long talk with Ted about giving some respite to Alice and her family by bringing the child to stay with them for a week or so. Just until Alice was back on her feet and could look after Clara herself, she told him.

Ted wasn't keen and Mrs Williams certainly wasn't. They both thought they had been more than accommodating, having Alice to stay with them for so long where the calm of the household had been compromised. There was a stalemate for a few days but Kate could be very persuasive, especially after seeing the mayhem in her family's household. Alice sat in a chair, ignoring Clara's tiny cry while Mrs Stainbank was at the sink, attempting to wash nappies. She was exhausted even after a small amount of exertion, stopping every few minutes to catch her breath. There were pots on the table which hadn't been cleared away since breakfast, no fire set so it was fortunate the weather was not too inclement.

Peggy Stainbank looked at her eldest daughter with tired eyes but also relief that for a short while at least the cavalry had arrived.

"What's going on, mam?" Kate asked, picking Clara from the basket to find she was wet through to the sheets.

"I thought once she'd had the bairn, she would pick up and help out but she's worse than ever. I can't carry on, Kate. I'm feeling real bad again, lass," she told her. "I shouldn't be doing all this at my time of life."

"Alice, Alice, get this baby sorted out. When did you last feed her? Come on, look sharp." Kate passed Clara over to Alice who looked shocked to be handed the child but did as she was told.

Kate helped Mrs Stainbank to move to the table before putting the kettle on to heat the water to wash the pots. Rolling up her sleeves, she began scrubbing the cotton squares, rinsing and rinsing until the water ran clear. Her hands were blue with cold but she didn't have time to wait for the kettle to boil. By the time she had made a pot of tea and put the remaining hot water in the sink to soak the breakfast pots, Alice had finished with Clara. Taking the baby from Alice, Kate said, "Get those nappies on the line. It's a good drying day. Go on now."

Peggy Stainbank looked thankfully at her eldest daughter. "I'm worried about our Alice. She leaves that bairn to cry and cry, everyone's on edge, our nerves are frayed. I'm at the end of me tether with her."

"You'll have to tell her what to do, mam. She doesn't know. If you don't, you'll end up doing everything and that's not good for you or the baby," Kate replied as she stared at the quiet child in her arms. "What are you having for tea?"

"There's meat left from Sunday so I was going to boil some potatoes and make a pie. There's cabbage and carrots and onions to peel," her mother told her.

As Alice walked back in the door, Kate looked at the poor girl. She seemed so slight, her tiny breasts struggling to provide enough milk and she had a weariness about her which hadn't gone away, making her look old before her time.

"Right, Alice, there's a cup of tea. Once you've had that, get the chopping board out and get on and peel the veg. Mam's going to show you how to make pastry when you've done that."

The girl didn't answer but sat at the table with her, warming her hands around the cup for comfort.

Clara had fallen asleep in Kate's arms so she took her to the pram where at least Alice had changed the sheets. They were left in a heap on the floor so she picked them up, taking them to the bucket in the kitchen to soak.

LATER THAT EVENING, Kate was telling her husband about the state of the house and how she was worried about the health of her mam and the mental state of Alice. What she was most worried about though was the baby, Clara, who seemed to get no attention at all from Alice. They needed a break, she said, before someone lost their temper. Alice was just a child herself, she told him.

In the end, Ted relented, telling her she could bring the baby over for a few days, but not until Monday, mind, as there would be enough of them at home over the weekend to keep an eye on the child. He was adamant that he wasn't going to get involved in any shape or form. Clara would be Kate's responsibility and hers alone. It would only be for a short period of time so she wasn't to get too attached, he told her sternly. Mrs Williams shook her head in despair at the thought of yet more disruption in the house.

That was how it started. Kate collected Clara and her meagre belongings and brought her home in her son's pram. For the first few days, she wondered what she had let herself in for as the child whined and grizzled every time she was awake. She didn't visit her family, thinking it would be better to let them get used to things and have a break so it was Friday before she wrapped the baby in the shawl Mrs Williams had made for her, put her in the pram and walked to the house on the way over to the market. Edward was happy to walk alongside the pram. He would be starting school soon and the house would be empty without him.

Mrs Stainbank was still struggling with the after effects of the pneumonia but her eyes were no longer sunken in pain. The cough had abated though she still got short of breath when she went up the stairs or out in the colder air.

Both women seemed much happier, the house was certainly tidier and there was less friction. Kate thought it was odd that Alice didn't go into the yard to look at her sleeping daughter. The only remaining link she seemed to have with the child was that her breasts had been tightly strapped to stop her producing milk as Kate had put Clara onto a pap bottle.

As Clara remained with Kate, she began to thrive and became much more settled. However, her first smile was for Ted who against his better judgement was becoming besotted with her. He would look into the pram and Clara's hand reached to hold his finger, looking into his eyes knowingly. "I think this one's been here before, just look at her looking round with those big wide eyes," he would say to Kate or his mother who just shook her head.

On Sundays, unless the inclement weather kept them indoors, the family would walk to Albert Park with young Edward who would walk there but get a ride on his father's shoulders on the way home. They were like hundreds of other families who were making their way in the new town. Work was springing up at the steelworks, the docks, the railway, so houses were being built everywhere. People were busy, they had money to buy goods in the shops and markets so the whole area was thriving. The town was moving out to the villages beyond while accents from all over the country could be heard.

Sometimes John and Ellen, who had become his steady girlfriend, would join them. They had met when they moved to Middlesbrough and were in the same class at school. There had never been anyone else for either of them and their friendship blossomed as they got older. Kate loved her younger brother. He was kind and considerate if rather quiet. The death of Frank seemed to have affected him more than the others, she thought, because he was the only brother now and the stammer had started after Frank's death and had never gone away. Perhaps that was why he was quiet because he was embarrassed about it though it never stopped him being happy with Ellen. He loved spending time with Kate and her family, pushing his nephew on the swings or catching him off the slide, laughing as he threw the boy into the air. He also made a fuss of his niece who was a feisty child even though she was small for her age.

On New Year's Eve 1888, Kate invited everyone to hers for the celebration as she felt they should have something to celebrate after the terrible year they'd had, hoping the next one would be better. John brought Ellen as well as his prospective in-laws. Furniture was pushed back and the kitchen table was laden with food which everyone had provided. Neighbours came and went as the evening went on. Just before midnight, the men stepped out into the street as all the other households did the same. They waited for the toll of the bells on the town hall clock and the ships' hooters sounding on the Tees. The noise echoed along the streets as the first footer knocked on the door, a piece of coal in his hand. For some reason, the tradition dictated more good luck the darker the hair so Ted was the first through the door to let the New Year in and straight through to the back door to let the old year out.

Everyone hugged and kissed each other, hoping and

praying for a happy, healthy and peaceful new year. Glasses of beer were handed to the men who had now come into the house and food was piled onto plates in celebration. Kate looked around at her family, realising how lucky she was to have them all around her. Her father for a small man was always the life and soul of a party. He always had a story to tell which made everyone laugh and he always joined in the singing with Ted who still had that wonderful baritone voice. No one mentioned Frank, no one wanted to remember him. Rachel had been at a party in the town and had brought back a number of girl and boy friends to help celebrate. She was very much like her dad, Kate thought, something always seemed to happen to her which made a good story.

By the end of January, the weather was mild compared to the previous year but everyone was unsettled as though a storm was brewing. There were big changes in the Williams household when Kate realised she was pregnant again. Ted was delighted. They both thought it might never happen with their son being four years old. She had fallen pregnant with him shortly after their wedding so thought they would have had several babies by now. Clara was nine months old and had become a delightful child, her eyes following both her husband and son around like a shadow. She was still a tiny scrap of a child but she could be a madam, very determined to get her own way, screaming loudly if necessary.

Kate wanted to go along and tell her family the good news but was prevented by the morning sickness which seemed to affect her all day. She didn't want to leave the children with Mrs Williams either. She had never warmed to Clara. Edward on the other hand was the apple of her eye, her son's boy who was kind natured like his father. She didn't like to leave him out if she was going out with Clara in the pram and quite rightly so. Clara had remained in the Williams household, no one ever mentioned her returning to her mother, Alice. Well, certainly not Kate or Ted though Mrs Williams may have secretly wished it.

It was Friday of that week when John called round with news of his own. Kate thought he was going to tell her that he had proposed to Ellen and that she had accepted as they seemed so loved up at New Year.

He laughed when she pre-empted his news, saying she would be the first to know if that happened, after Ellen and her parents that was. But, no, the Linthorpe Pottery was to close unless a buyer could be found to put some money into it. The clay was drying up and they were having to transport it from Cornwall which was putting the price up, he said, making it too expensive.

After the initial shock and the usual questions – what would he do? what about their father's work? – questions which John couldn't answer, he told her he was still attempting to take in the news himself. Any thought of marrying Ellen would have to wait until he found himself another job, John told them.

The one bit of good news was Kate's pregnancy and he was happy to pass the news on for her. Hugging his sister tightly, John felt as though his life was due to change forever but he would always have Kate on his side. Once or twice, he had thought to confess to her about the murder of Frank to salve his own conscience but it was his mother who had made him promise on her life that he would never tell anyone, not even Ellen. It's your burden, she had told him, you have to live with it as best you can, don't put it on anyone else.

When Kate and Ted were alone, when Mrs Williams had retired for the night and the children long since in their beds, they talked about what John had said. Luckily for them, Ted worked in the steelworks which was booming. "Do you think you would be able to get either or both a job," she asked hopefully.

"I could ask but I don't know if your father would thank me," Ted replied. "He's a master craftsman so wouldn't think too kindly to having to start again. I might be able to ask about John though. I will see what I can do. He's a grafter your John, I'll say that for him."

"Yes, I know. Remember when our Frank was killed? He really struggled for a while even though they weren't close. Well, no one was close to our Frank. Suddenly John was the eldest son and that was a big responsibility for him. He was always a quiet lad and somehow overshadowed when he was a bairn," Kate said almost whimsically.

"Aye, well, they were two different characters, that's for sure. John has always been kind, boy and man. Ellen will be lucky to have him as a husband," Ted laughed.

"That was almost romantic, Ted Williams, and that's why I love you." Kate went into his arms.

"Who's being romantic now, Kate Williams? I love you too. Now come on, let's stop being all soppy and get to bed." He slapped her playfully on the backside.

IT HAD BEEN in the local paper about the problems at Linthorpe Pottery and everyone employed there. By the end of May 1889, the pottery closed with approximately one hundred people losing their jobs. Some of the younger men found work on the river or the steelworks which had sprung up everywhere. John had been fortunate to be taken on by Dorman Long at South Bank but he hated it. Mr Stainbank had not been so lucky. Now in his fifties, he didn't want 'a bit of a lad' telling him what to do. He got under his wife's feet, sitting doing nothing all day. He had reluctantly gone to the parish to see if they could get any help but they were refused because both Rachel and John were working. He would tell anyone who would listen that even though they had lived in Middlesbrough for ten years they couldn't get help because it wasn't the parish they had been born in.

Rachel had worked for a number of years for Dr Hylton and his wife as a sort of carer and companion. She liked it because she didn't have to live in and she didn't work on a Saturday and was free all day Sunday. It meant she could go out for a concert or dancing with her friends. She was probably the most sociable one of the family, enjoying her life and determined that she wasn't going to get married too soon, even if anyone asked her, which they hadn't. She never seemed to keep a boyfriend for long, they got too serious and she just wanted to go out and enjoy herself, not save her money to buy items for a house. No, she wasn't envious of Kate… she was just having a good time.

KATE WAS surprised when they were all invited to her parents' house for Sunday lunch because there wasn't much room in the kitchen. They all walked over together. Mrs Williams had tried to get out of it, saying they could plate up her lunch and bring it back, but Kate refused, saying the invite was for all of them and it would be churlish not to accept.

They didn't say much while they were eating, roast lamb, cooked slowly in the bottom of the oven while they were at church, so it fell off the bone. Roast potatoes, cabbage, carrots and Yorkshire pudding. The latter was served first with lashings of gravy to fill their hungry bellies. Rachel chuntered as she was told to do the washing up with Alice while the others went into the lounge, John bringing in a dining chair to sit on.

Mr Stainbank stood, clearing his throat. "Well lass," he looked at Kate, "Mr Roth had offered me a position, that's what he called it," he chuckled to himself, "a position and I've accepted."

"That's good news, dad. I'm really pleased for you, honestly I am. It's about time we had some good news."

"Let me finish, lass. Aye, you're right, it is good news but it's back in Stafford so we are going to have to move there. Rachel's not happy about it, she wants to stay here but Alice will come back with us."

"Well, Rachel can't stay with us. There's little enough room as it is and what about Clara? Are you taking her with you?" Kate said loudly. "She's settled with us now. Ted, tell them."

"I know Clara thinks of you as her mam and dad and she's settled. It would be a fresh start for our Alice if the child stayed with you. We're not asking you to take Rachel in, lass. She was going to ask Dr Hylton if she could live in but that would curb her gallivanting, that's for sure. Anyroad, we wanted to tell you straight away like 'cause we'll be going in a few weeks," Peggy Stainbank said in a matter of fact way which annoyed Kate.

"Aw mam, you won't be here when I have the bairn. What do you say about Clara, Alice? Are you happy for her to stay here with us? Some people seem to forget she is your daughter." Kate was on the verge of tears at the thought, hoping and praying that she wouldn't want the child back.

Alice just shrugged her shoulders, as though she hadn't given the little mite any thought.

"There's no need for that, Kate. It can't be helped, lass. If you don't want to keep Clara, of course we'll take her with us but you know as I said it would be a fresh start for our Alice. Anyroad, that's not the only news. Come on, John, don't be shy." Mr Stainbank looked at his son, trying to sway the conversation away from them for a short while at least.

Kate looked at her brother who she hoped, prayed, wasn't going to leave as well. He wouldn't leave Ellen behind, she was sure.

"Ellen's p- p- p- parents have relatives in N- N- New

Zealand," he said, taking a deep breath. "He ha- he ha- he has offered to put us up until we get on our f- f- feet." John stammered more when he was het up.

Kate couldn't take it in. Her parents moving hundreds of miles and now John saying he was going to the other side of the world. She hardly heard what he said next.

"The b- b- banns will be read f- f- for the first time on Sunday so we will ma- ma- marry just before mam and dad move. Be happy for me, Kate."

"I am happy for you, John. You were made for each other but why go to the end of the world? Can't you be happy here?" She was crying now, large tears rolling down her face at the enormity of what everyone was saying. "You could find a better job here. Ted will find one for you. Tell him, Ted."

"Look, love, John has to make his own decisions. He's a grown man. He'll have Ellen with him so he won't be on his own. I know it's hard but let's celebrate a wedding." Ted was patting her hand.

"Stop that blathering, Kate, you'll upset that bairn you're carrying," Mrs Williams said sternly. "Stop crying, for goodness sake, you with your incontinence problems, water will be coming out from both ends."

Kate laughed loudly, in spite of being so upset. "Oh, you do have a turn of phrase, you do. I'll be wetting myself alright with laughter." The mood was broken as they all laughed though they all knew it wasn't with any real joy and happiness.

Rachel came in with a tray of tea and biscuits and beer for the men. "Told you their news, have they?" she said, sneering. "I've told 'em I ain't going, leaving all my friends behind and my job. I've said I ain't going."

Mrs Stainbank looked at her daughter. "Where are you going to live then, miss, tell me that? You don't earn enough to rent a place of your own."

"Why can't our Kate move here? There's more room with

the loft," Rachel spat, looking at her sister. "I'd be happy to sleep up there and she could have the other bedrooms."

"Forget that, our Rachel. I don't want to move here. I'm happy where I am. We wouldn't fit in anyway once I've had the bairn. It'll be a tight squeeze in our own place." Kate couldn't believe her cheek.

"Aye and I'll end up in the box room for me sins," Mrs Williams stated, somewhat sarcastically though no one was listening to what she had to say.

"You could rent a bigger house and I'd chip in with the rent, then we'd all have a room." Rachel glared at Mrs Williams.

"I'm saying no more about it. We're not moving so that's that," Kate told her, nodding to her mother-in-law.

"Ch- ch- ch- changing the subject, Ted wo- wo- would you be my best man?" John asked, trying to stop the arguing.

"I'd be honoured, lad, really I would." Ted beamed at John.

As they walked home, Kate pushing Clara in the pram, Ted put his hand on hers. "It's been quite a day, hasn't it?"

CHAPTER 18

The weeks leading up to the wedding were hectic as the Stainbanks were busy trying to sort out what they were taking to Stafford with them. Everyone was unsettled and none more so than Kate who felt she was losing everyone she loved, apart from Ted and her son and Clara of course. She had argued with her mother over what would happen to Clara. After all, Kate said, she was only supposed to be with her on a temporary arrangement. However, she didn't want to make too much of it because she couldn't bear the thought of losing the child, and she didn't need to ask Ted as he felt the same.

The wedding was a somewhat muted affair for two reasons. The first was obviously to do with John's parents moving back to Stafford but also because they were not observing the twelve months of mourning after Frank's death.

The police had never charged anyone with his murder, for which John was grateful as he did not want an innocent man on his conscience as well as his brother's demise.

Ellen was delighted that they were to marry. Like John, she was a quiet natured, happy soul. She was excited at the thought of starting a new life with him on the other side of the world. She had been surprised that he had agreed to the move as she always thought he would have preferred to have either stayed where Kate and her family were or move with his parents. Kate had loaned her the cornflower blue dress and Ellen had attached lace to the neckline as well as around the skirt to make a train. It was a small wedding with only the immediate family invited. The men dressed in their only suits while the women wore their Sunday best. The only additions were lace gloves and flowers sewn around the crowns of their bonnets.

The bride and groom asked that no gifts be purchased so both families agreed to pay for two nights stay in a hotel before going to Ellen's parents for the few weeks before their journey to New Zealand. Kate gave John one of the Linthorpe Pottery vases that had been given to her as a wedding present. It stood only eight inches tall and it was one of her first pieces she had designed and completed. Its colours were, from the bottom, green with a fern leaf pattern changing to an orange or burnt gold in the middle. The flute at the top was mustard in colour. Her initials KS were underneath with Christopher Dresser's initials alongside. Kate told him she would keep the other one in the hope that one day they would be re-united and each time she looked at it, she would think of them.

John had furnished Ted with money to pay the wedding expenses as they sat in church waiting for the bride and father to arrive. He stood at the altar, watching Ellen and her father walk slowly down the aisle where she stood to the left of him. He managed to say his vows without too much stuttering even though he was very nervous. There was an awkward pause as Ellen struggled to remove her glove so the ring could be placed on her finger, and a titter went around the attendees.

Ellen's parents arranged a reception at their home where

the women had been baking for days. Mr Stainbank provided a barrel of ale and a bottle of brandy to toast the newly-weds. The party carried on long after the married couple had left for the hotel.

Kate looked around the room at her family. How she would miss them all but especially her mam and John whom she had grown very close to. It was strange how she hadn't had a lot to do with Rachel over the years as she seemed to have been overshadowed by Alice's problems. Watching her now, Kate realised that she had grown up. She was confident talking to Ellen's relatives, even joining in with the men, laughing loudly.

Ted and her father were deep in conversation, both with rosy cheeks from the drink. Mr Stainbank tapped a knife against his glass, telling everyone the singing was about to start. Ted began, his voice deep and clear, followed by the other men.

She was moved almost to tears. She was so proud of her husband, but it was time to go home, the children were asleep but that was fine… she'd expected as much and had dropped the pram off earlier in the day. She would walk home with the children and Mrs Williams, leaving Ted to his singing and hangover.

AFTER THE JOY and happiness of the wedding the week before, Kate's heart was almost breaking as she said goodbye to her family. She clung to her parents as though her life depended on it, sobbing into Ted's shoulder as she watched them board the train. Edward and Clara had been left with Mrs Williams and she knew she couldn't delay her return for too long or there might be murder done. John and Ellen agreed to walk back to the house with them for a bite to eat. They all wanted to remain together for as long as possible.

Rachel didn't go to Stafford with her family but had

enrolled on a nursing course in Durham after Dr Hylton had given her a glowing reference. She promised to write to Kate when she had time to let her know how she was getting on.

Kate's pregnancy was progressing well, though her emotional state made her feel frightened to look too far into the future. In four weeks' time, she would have to say goodbye to her brother who she was sure she would never see again.

Kate had brought the children to the station with her this time. Mrs Williams couldn't cope with madam Clara, who tormented Edward until she ended up with a smack. Kate hugged John, making him promise to write as soon as they arrived to let her know he was safe. She stood on the platform until the train was out of sight, tears leaving sooty tracks down her face. Even as Ted passed his handkerchief, she couldn't speak, couldn't imagine life without her family. But imagine it she must, her family was here, Ted, her son and Clara. This was all there was now… oh and her mother-in-law.

By early September, the house had become very quiet. Ted was at work and Edward had started school, leaving Kate in the house with Mrs Williams and Clara. She set to cleaning everything in sight while the weather held. Bedding was washed, curtains hung out to air, carpets hung up and beaten. It stopped her becoming maudlin or having time to think. As she beat the carpets, dust floating in the air, she blamed Frank for all that seemed to have gone wrong with her life. For that brief moment she forgot about the good things, the happy times. With each negative thought, the carpets were given a thorough beating which was in a way cathartic to her, cleansing both her mind and the carpets.

She walked for miles, pushing Clara in the pram, first to take Edward to school then up to the village on market day.

Everywhere, women with children were buying goods as the town grew. Linthorpe itself seemed like a town, houses being built everywhere, the nearby countryside almost gone as they linked up with the hamlet of Acklam.

They squeezed the cot into her son's bedroom which wasn't ideal, with the deep drawer in their bedroom ready for the new baby. Kate had spoken to Ted about his mother swapping from the slightly larger room but she refused to even broach the subject, saying she needed a sanctuary where she could escape the madness of the house. So that was that. Kate certainly wasn't going to broach the subject with her mother-in-law.

She went into early labour at thirty-four weeks and she knew it was just too soon. One of the neighbours went for the midwife who rolled up her sleeves, telling her not to push, but it was no good, the baby wouldn't wait. Something wasn't right, she could feel it and the midwife confirmed it, saying the doctor needed to be called as it was breach. Ted rushed off while Kate yelled in absolute agony, holding on tightly to the headboard. The midwife realised the child wasn't breach but that the placenta was coming away first. She yelled to Mrs Williams to boil plenty of water while more towels would be needed. By the time the doctor arrived, Kate had lost a lot of blood but the placenta was in a bowl while the child was struggling to be born.

Several hours later, her son was finally silently born, no struggling to breathe, he was grey and limp. He had died in the womb which was supposed to protect him. Kate was too tired to cry while her son was wrapped in a pillowcase to be taken away. There would be no birth certificate, no funeral, no grave, it was as though he had never existed. But for Kate, he had been her child, her much wanted child. The doctor took his leave, taking her baby with him but before he left, Kate shouted. He was to be called David, his name was David.

The midwife indicated that Ted could now come into the bedroom and with his arms around her, Kate fell into a deep exhausted sleep.

Life went on but there was an ache in Kate's arms, while her breasts produced milk for no hungry soul to drink. She couldn't talk even to Ted about David as it was too raw for both of them. The pain left her numb until she couldn't feel anything anymore. How she wished the same could be said for her mind. She was grateful for Edward and Clara, vowing to try and get into her stride for them. She missed the company of her mother, she missed the conversations and that her mother would know what to say. Mrs Williams was kindly if a somewhat plain speaking woman but over the years Kate had warmed to her brusque manner. Still, it wasn't the same as talking to your own family.

Kate felt her family would now be complete with Edward and Clara. She felt in her heart that she would never have another child. She saw others having one after another and they would have welcomed a houseful of children but it wasn't to be.

Ted was earning a good wage as a furnace keeper, almost £3 per week. It was his job to keep the furnace in working order so no days were lost. He often came home with steel burns where the sudden jet of vivid flame came over the top of the furnace. His face and arms particularly had what appeared to be dirt marks. No amount of scrubbing or cleaning lightened the shade and it gave him an older face. When Kate had first met him, he looked almost boyish even though he was five years older than her, but now his skin had a grey hue.

Once Clara started talking, she never stopped and her disobedience disappeared at the same time. She asked question after question, why, when, how, it seemed without pausing for breath. She finally managed to endear herself to Mrs Williams as she would sit with her to listen to a story, though woe betide Mrs Williams if she changed a word as Clara could remember them all. She also looked forward to Edward coming home from school when they played together in the yard.

Kate wondered if the trauma of Clara's birth had made her such a fiery character or the early days when her mother had almost abandoned her. Now she was in a settled household with plenty of love and attention, she had thrived both mentally and physically, though she was still small for her age.

All in all, Kate thought her life was going well although she would never forget David. They would never be rich but had enough to feed and clothe their family. She was frugal with her spending, though no one could say Ted was anything other than generous. They managed to save something each week, the coins going into the vase on the mantelpiece. Whenever she touched it, and she often did, she thought of the other one with John and Ellen on the other side of the world, wondering what they were doing and if they were thinking of her.

The seasons seemed to come and go as the years went by. Kate received letters occasionally from both her family in Stafford and Ellen in New Zealand. She kept them in a small wooden box which had a metal lock and key, though it was never locked, she had nothing to hide from her husband. Kate had become friendly with Ellen's mother who she visited with Clara to give Mrs Williams a bit of quiet time while Edward was at school. If the weather was fine, they would walk to the park so Clara could let off steam.

Clara looked nothing like her mother. Her hair wasn't blonde though not as dark as Kate's and certainly not as black as Ted and Edward's. Her features were dainty. She looked much too small to be starting school and her school dress had to be altered to fit but what she lacked in stature she made up for in keenness to join in everything. Edward played the big brother, shepherding her through the school gate. Kate was a little tearful as she watched the two of them disappear into the old building. Neither had looked round or waved goodbye.

The house seemed empty and quiet. She wondered if now could be a good time to apply for her teaching certificate. She would speak to Ted as to his opinion on the matter. She wouldn't be able to work in a local school but might be able to do private tutoring in time.

ANOTHER CHRISTMAS and New Year of 1892 came and went as life went on for Kate. She learned that John and Ellen had had a second daughter, Christa, two years after Elodi, who was the image of John. They now had their own wood-built cottage on the land belonging to Ellen's family and there was room to extend if their family grew even further. John was happy out on the land all day, looking after what seemed like hundreds of sheep. He had two dogs of his own and they walked miles every day. Ellen was grateful, they both were, to have been given the opportunity. Her relatives had no family so the land would pass to John. They had already prepared an affidavit, but she prayed that it wouldn't be needed for a long time. She talked about the lambing season and how John could be up all night if one of the ewes was in difficulty and some of the lambs were hand reared in the kitchen which their eldest daughter Elodi loved feeding. Although he looked as though a puff of wind would blow him over, John was a strong man.

Kate always read the letters to Mrs Williams and again to Ted, saying how happy she was for them all and how it would be nice to go and see them, knowing that would never happen. Her life seemed mundane so when Ted told her that his works were organising a charabanc trip to the seaside and he was going to pay for them all to go on the day out, she was delighted. Mrs William's wasn't sure if she wanted to go but her son told her they would all go or no one. Edward and Clara begged and pleaded until she relented.

So here they were in the middle of August, in their Sunday best, walking up New Cemetery Road to the village. Kate had packed sandwiches, towels, a blanket and a flask of tea as well as a bottle of water for the children. Enough for a week, Ted told her laughing. The children were trying to hurry Mrs Williams along in case they missed the transport but she only had one speed, slow.

It seemed half the town was going. Ted looked at his ticket. They were on bus number three so they all piled on, taking up a whole bench to themselves. As the charabanc set off, it jerked forward. People nervously laughed, shuffling in their seats. Clara sat by the window with Edward standing in front of her, then Kate next, then Mrs Williams, with Ted edging himself precariously on the edge of the seat with the bag at his feet.

There was much excitement as the houses gave way to the countryside before someone shouted they could see the sea. There was a mass exodus as they spilt out onto the sand. Ted found a spot, laying out the blanket before helping his mother unceremoniously drop to the sand, legs akimbo, showing off her undergarments which went past her knees, her hat skewiff, making her look like a drunken harlot. Kate tried to smother her laughter, failing, as she laughed out loud. Ted joined in along with the children though Mrs Williams didn't seem to find the humour.

Kate removed her shoes and stockings, picking up her skirt and running down to the sea to catch up with Ted and the children where they were squealing as the cold water covered their feet and ankles. Although the sun was beating down, there was a cool breeze off the sea which made it much cooler. Taking Ted's hand, she thought how lucky she was as they eventually walked back up to the blanket for their picnic. Sand crunched between their teeth when they ate their egg sandwiches and no matter how many times they rubbed their feet with the towel, sand remained in their shoes for days.

Within minutes of the charabanc setting off for home, the children and even some of the adults were asleep. The men began the singing, harmonies perfect on the ears as they held an impromptu choir practice. Kate, as usual, loved to hear the richness of all the voices but especially Ted's.

All too soon, the days returned to the routine of normality but the children often talked about the seaside with the promise they could go again the following year. The trip had taken a lot out of Mrs Williams and Kate was worried about her health, though she never seemed to ail anything apart from getting older.

CHAPTER 19

It was late Monday morning in October 1894 just as Kate was hanging washing on the line that she heard the dull boom in the distance, not once but twice. It could have been thunder but the way the air seemed to be sucked from around her, she knew it was from the steelworks.

"Did you hear that?" she asked Mrs Williams as she returned indoors.

"All the windows rattled. It sounds bad," her mother-in-law replied.

Kate opened the front door to see her neighbours looking skyward where there was a thin reed of black smoke rising high into the air like a long charcoal pencil. The women moved into a loose huddle as if for support, waiting, watching, mumbling to one another. Do you think we should go to the works? one asked, while another said, no, they would be in the way. Someone will come and tell us soon enough, another said as they hoped and prayed they wouldn't get the knock.

Ted was late home but Kate kept telling herself he would

be staying behind to help with the injured or to dig out anyone caught under the debris. She wished she had gone along to the gates. She would have known more there.

Kate and Mrs Williams jumped when there was a loud rapping at the front door. They looked toward each other, neither wanting to speak as Kate quietly closed the door to the hallway before opening the front door. She knew before the man spoke that it wasn't good news. He was covered in soot, his voice hoarse.

"I'm sorry, Mrs Williams, there's been an accident," he rasped. "Your husband has been taken to the cottage hospital on Westbourne Grove with severe burns. I'm so sorry."

As she leaned against the door jam, she felt her knees buckle. All she could say was, "At least he's alive, thank you for letting me know."

The poor man moved a few doors along, hammering on another poor family's door. She felt faint but Ted needed her. She had to get to the hospital.

Hurrying into the room, she quickly told Mrs Williams what she knew while she put on her coat and bonnet. "Get yerself away, lass. The bairns will be alright. Go on now. I'll say a prayer for him."

Kate wanted to scream at the woman. Prayers were no good, her husband wasn't going to die. The man had got it wrong, it wouldn't be so bad.

Almost at a run up New Cemetery Road, Kate almost stepped out in front of a cab as she rushed to cross the road in the village. She continued down the side of the park and it was almost dark when she reached the hospital. There were people standing around everywhere. Men still in their work clothes, smoking, while the women just seemed to be in a trance. Kate went toward a man holding a sheet of paper.

"I'm looking for Ted, Edward Williams? I'm his wife." She looked at him but he continued to look at his piece of paper as he ushered her through the hospital door and into a corridor where the smell of burnt flesh almost made her want to gag. Men were laid on stretchers, groaning, reaching out for help as she walked past.

He spoke to one of the nurses who was hurrying by who simply said, "Follow me."

The man returned to his station by the door. They paused by a bed where someone seemed to be covered from head to foot in bandages. This can't be Ted, Kate cried inside, but the nurse said quietly, "I'll see if I can find you a chair. The doctor will be along as soon as he can." With that, she hurried off to tend to someone else.

She couldn't take Ted's hand so spoke to him softly in the hope he knew she was there. How long she sat she didn't know but was awoken with a start when she heard a voice by the bed. It was the doctor who looked exhausted as he pushed his hair out of his eyes.

"Your husband is in a bad way, Mrs Williams. We have cleaned him up as best we can and he has been given something for the pain so he will be out of it for some time, I'm afraid. I suggest you go home and get some sleep. We won't know anything for the next few days."

"No, I can't leave him. I need to be here in case he wakes up." She was exhausted but didn't want to go home. "What time is it?" she asked, realising she had been asleep for some time.

"It's almost one in the morning. Look, I'll try and find you a cup of tea," the nurse said before the two of them moved on to the next bed to attend the next patient.

Kate sat until it was time to get the children up for school. She would have to go home to try and make things look normal for them and to let Mrs Williams know how her son was but she would come straight back.

. . .

KATE TOOK the children to school. They asked questions but she brushed them off, saying their dad was in hospital but would soon be home. She hoped that would be true even if she had to nurse him herself.

Her bones ached as she sat in the kitchen, trying to explain to her mother-in-law what had happened. The rumour was a blow back in the furnace, four were known to be dead with twenty eight or so injured. Ted was in a bad way and covered in bandages. She tried to think what the doctor had told her, that the next few days would be critical but she needed to get back. If she wasn't back to pick the children up from school, one of the neighbours would go, she said, as she left the house again.

It was five days later that Ted took a turn for the worse. The doctor thought his mother should be brought so Kate made the decision to get a cab back to the house to collect Mrs Williams who would never have walked all the way to the hospital. She would be able to drop the children off at Ellen's parents on the way, who agreed to keep them for however long it took. The words hung in the air as she ran back to the cab and onto the hospital. When she climbed down, she proffered her money to the driver who turned it down saying, "You need it more than me, Mrs." She thanked him tearfully before going through the hospital doors.

Kate had tried to warn her mother-in-law of the terrible state of the men but all she could hear was "Oh dear God" as they went into the ward. There were beds almost on top of each other as the nurses moved awkwardly amongst them.

Mrs Williams sat in the chair close to Ted's head while Kate stood on the other side. He was agitated, groaning but she couldn't help. As his arms moved slightly, she could smell the disease, the infection on his burns which was slowly killing him. The doctor gave him another sedative but all the two women could do was wait. Kate paced up and down the side of the bed, wanting to pull her husband into her arms so he knew she was there but she talked softly to him instead.

Kate was surprised when Mrs Williams cleared her throat and began to sing, quietly at first as her voice wobbled before she got into full flow. She had never heard her sing before, surprised at how clear her voice was. As she finished, she looked tearfully at her daughter-in-law. "If my boy's going to die, I want him to hear the sound of his own country."

Kate couldn't respond but took Ted's bandaged hand gently as Mrs Williams continued her songs one after the other. How long this continued she wasn't sure but when the nurse came to check, she said, "I'm sorry, he's gone."

"No, no, no," Kate groaned, falling to her knees. Both women wailed as the rest of the world seemed to be going about its business. The nurse came back and managed to squeeze screens around the bed so they had some privacy. "Stay as long as you like."

She couldn't take it in. Her husband was the mainstay of the family, he drew them together with his sparkling eyes and easy manner. His Welsh lilt had softened over the years but when he sang, his chest swelled with pride at where he came from. She would hear that voice no more. The only man she had ever loved was gone. Kate couldn't bear it. She was a widow with two children and a mother-in-law depending on her. Her poor husband was only thirty five, no age at all. He would never see his children grow up, never walk Clara down the aisle on her wedding day. She stopped herself from thinking like this, it was too painful. She would have to try and get through the next few days and weeks for the sake of the children. Looking around the hospital ward, she knew she wouldn't be the only wife or mother to feel this sense of absolute desolation.

Kate and Mrs Williams didn't speak of their feelings. What could they say? Both would have to mourn in their own way.

The doctor at the hospital signed the death certificate and because of the risk of illness to the family and the smell of Ted's body, he could not be taken back to the house to be laid out but would have to remain at the hospital until the funeral.

She was glad of that as the coffin would have had to be placed on two chairs in the cramped living room with a black tablecloth over. She had worried what effect it would have on the children. They probably would have had nightmares.

Silently, the two women drew the curtains in all the rooms, the mantelpiece clock stopped at the time of his death and the mirror covered over. The latter wasn't really necessary. With Ted's body not being in the house, his spirit wasn't there to be trapped in the mirror. However, Kate didn't have the energy to argue.

A wreath with black crepe fastened around it was hung on the front door to alert visitors of a death, though everyone knew. The neighbours rallied round, someone brought a casserole, another went to the post office to send telegrams to Kate's family and Mrs Williams' brother, as another offered to take Edward and Clara to school. She wasn't the only one in the street to be affected and the community came together at these times.

She counted out the money from the vase. It wouldn't last long with all the bills to pay. Kate put her head in her hands. She would have to find employment or they would end up in the workhouse. How long she could continue to pay the rent she didn't know. The knocking on the front door brought her out of her thoughts as a gentleman from the works was shown in.

His name was David Evans, Di to his friends. After offering Kate his condolences and his hand, they sat for a moment until she could compose herself.

"What happened to my husband?" she asked.

"We are not sure other than there was a blowback from the furnace. The charge was complete and the contents lowered into the blast furnace. We don't know if the constitution of the charge was incorrect or whether something fell in but a huge jet of flame blew out, catching the men in the way," he told her with his head down. "What I came to tell you, Mrs Williams, is that your husband paid into two funds from his wages. He paid into the cottage hospital funds at North Ormesby where he was taken. This was to pay for his care should there be an accident and that money will be paid direct to the hospital so there is no need to worry about that. The other was two pence a week on a life insurance policy which will pay for his funeral. I have two five pound notes here for you. The men at the works have had a collection for those who died and I have another ten shillings here." He placed four half crowns on top of the notes. "I wish I could offer more." He shook his head as his voice trailed off.

She looked at the money but it was no consolation.

The next day it was the vicar who called when all Kate wanted to do was to be left alone with her grief but she talked to him about Ted's funeral. The total cost of the funeral would be five pounds which included the pall bearers and a funeral cart pulled by one black horse. She handed over one of the notes. There would be no money for a headstone, she knew that.

When Rachel and Mr Stainbank arrived later that week, she flew into her dad's arms, crying out with such pain.

"How are you bearing up, lass?" he asked.

"I'm still breathing in and out. If it wasn't for the children, well…" Kate wiped away the tears.

"We'll have none of that, Kate. You've got to be strong, especially over the next few days," Rachel said, surprising her. Her younger sister would now be twenty five and very grown up and sure of herself. "Have you eaten today?"

Shaking her head, Kate told her she wasn't hungry but Rachel was having none of it. There wasn't much food in the house so she put some eggs on to boil for them all before slicing what was left of the bread as thinly as possible.

Mr Stainbank and Rachel were staying with Ellen's parents so there was a small space for Mrs Williams' brother and his wife if everyone shuffled round. Kate had never met them before, finding it difficult to make them welcome when all she wanted was to be left alone. Their voices reminded her so much of Ted that it was a physical pain in her chest.

The dreaded day arrived with the children being sent to school. Ellen's mother was remaining at the house to prepare food and tea for the wake. They had arranged the funeral for four o'clock so that the early shift from the steelworks would be able to attend and those on the night shift would at least get some sleep. Kate was surprised, shocked even, at how many people attended her husband's funeral. Men in their work clothes, those from the choir, neighbours and friends all joined the family to walk behind Ted's coffin. She held on tightly to her dad while Mrs Williams was flanked by her brother and his wife. Kate felt as though the life she knew had been erased. She would never know that feeling of contentment and love again. How lucky she had been when she met and married Ted. The choir raised their voices to the heavens for the hymns which had been requested by Mrs Williams and it was very moving.

The men followed the coffin to the cemetery where those killed would be laid to rest in a corner. They hoped eventually to raise enough money to place a plaque or a stone in memory of those who had died in the accident.

Kate and the women returned to the house, sitting around the table, no one really knowing what to say. It was Rachel who broke the silence, talking about her work as a nurse which she had trained for when she moved to Durham, explaining how she worked on the wards during the day rather than nights, though quiet time gave her the chance to study for her exams. Kate nodded, the other women asked her sister questions about her life, and Kate was relieved that she didn't need to talk.

She was glad when the mourners had gone home and the children were in bed in her room. They had been unsettled but well behaved of which she was thankful. She came back to the present when Rachel asked why she didn't just pack up and go back with their father, at least she would have her family around her. But she couldn't, it was too soon, her husband had just been buried. Her life was here in Middlesbrough, the children were happy in school so she just shook her head in reply.

However, it was Mrs Williams who threw Kate completely. She declared that she would be returning to the hills of her country with her brother as there was nothing left for her here. Those were her exact words, and Kate couldn't believe it.

"Nothing for you here? What about Edward? What about your son's grave?" She was mortified at her mother-in-law's seeming disregard for everything Kate held dear.

"You'll see it's for the best with one less mouth to feed. I don't want to stay in this town. I want to die in Wales. My decision is made and it's final." With that, Mrs Williams took herself off into her room.

For Kate, her life seemed to be unravelling before her eyes. She would have to move to a smaller house, find a job just to keep them alive. It was too much. She was racked with sobs, broken hearted at the predicament she now found herself in. Rachel held her, telling her not to rush into anything. She could move to Stafford at any time. If Kate wanted, she could stay a little longer but she said no, she had to get on with things.

Within the next few days, the house became unusually quiet. Her father and Rachel had returned home and now the cart had arrived to take Mrs Williams, her brother and his wife to the station.

Kate hugged the old woman with a feeling of resentment and relief in equal measure. Resentment that she could leave her to her suffering alone, but also relief for the same reason. She didn't want to have to make polite conversation to her husband's mother, her dead husband's mother. Kate stood on the front step, her shawl wrapped tightly around her shoulders as she sighed deeply. Looking up to the sky, there was snow in the air.

She decided to walk to the village for vegetables for the evening meal, resisting the urge to visit Ted's grave. that was for another day. By the time she got back to the house, she had a little colour in her cheeks. Hugging Edward and Clara to her when they returned from school, she told them how proud she was of them and they would now have to help each other.

Surprisingly, she laughed when Edward said he would look for a job which he could do before school and at weekends, though she realised he may have to. Clara also offered her help so Kate told her she could start with the washing up.

Over the next few weeks, she tried to keep herself busy, cleaning out Mrs Williams' old room ready for Clara to move into. It served two purposes. She didn't have to think and it saved her putting the fire on until just before the children got home. She would miss the warmth of Clara's body in her bed. She had moved in while Ted was in hospital, and never moved out.

Kate wasn't looking forward to sleeping alone but Clara was excited at finally getting a room to herself.

They were about to sit down to their evening meal when there was a knock on the front door. They didn't have many visitors, people had left them to deal with their grief. Edward stepped through the living room, returning with Mr Evans who had removed his hat and gloves.

"Oh, I can see you are just about to sit down to your meal so I'll be quick," he said.

"Why don't you join us? Edward, take Mr Evans' coat. Clara, get another plate from the cupboard. I won't take no for an answer." Kate proffered him a seat.

"Mrs Williams not well?" He looked around the small kitchen.

"She decided to return to Wales so it's just the three of us now," Kate said sadly. "What brought you out on such a grim night, Mr Evans?"

"I could smell your wonderful food from down the street and thought it would be much better than the meagre offering at my lodgings." Mr Evans laughed and they all joined in. "No, no, to be serious for a minute, the reason I called is that the choir have arranged a concert for the beginning of December to raise funds for those who died in the blast." He looked at Kate. "I don't want to upset you but wondered if you would like to come along."

"Can we, mam?" Clara asked.

"No, I don't think so," Kate replied, thinking she would never be able to sit and listen to the wonderful Welsh voices ever again.

"I see, I thought it might be too soon but I wanted to ask you personally. Now I've taken up enough of your time, filled myself up on your lovely meal so I'll be on my way." Mr Evans said goodnight to Edward and Clara.

As Kate saw him out, he took her hand. "I'm so sorry for your loss, Mrs Williams. Ted was a good man. If you ever need anything please let me know." Then he was gone.

By the time she returned to the kitchen, the bread had gone. They had wiped it round their plates.

"They won't need washing up," she laughed. "You haven't even left a crust for me."

Leading up to Christmas was a sad time but Kate took them to the market in the village where they shared a bag of warm chestnuts. She bought both of them a pair of woollen gloves, while they were watching the juggler. She had never been able to understand the basics of knitting.

Kate was still wearing black but she didn't want the house to become a mausoleum so had decided to buy some coloured paper to make decorations, though this year they wouldn't be having a big celebration nor would she be having a New Year party. Both Edward and Clara said they didn't want anything for Christmas, for which she was grateful. The money wouldn't last much longer so she knew she would have to find a job of some description in the New Year. She didn't really know what she could do. She had only ever worked in the pottery and then she married Ted. She did have her school certificate but she wanted to be in when the children got home from school. Something would turn up but she would get the festive season out of the way before worrying any more.

CHRISTMAS WAS a sombre affair with a meagre assortment of food and very little in the way of gifts but the children didn't complain. If Kate had been alone, she would have remained in bed for the holidays, in her own company, but she did the best she could for Edward and Clara. For Kate, the days were long but she tried to get out of the house as much as she could. It saved on heating and the walks brought a colour to their cheeks.

She was relieved when the New Year bells rang out for 1895, a new start in more ways than one. There was a depression in the town so any kind of work was almost impossible to find and if there was, employers preferred to hire men to keep families out of the workhouse. The rate she was spending money would put them in there if she didn't do something soon.

One of the neighbours suggested she take in a lodger but Kate wasn't keen. The only person she could think of was Mr Evans but didn't know how to contact him. The children had warmed to him but didn't feel comfortable with someone who had known Ted and she didn't want a stranger. However Kate knew she would have to do something when the rent was increased by tuppence a week.

CHAPTER 20

Kate walked into town, becoming more and more depressed as she got the same answer in all the shops and establishments. No work was to be had. She felt as though she was prostituting herself as her begging for work became desperate. She had almost walked the length of Linthorpe Road when she called into a shop selling shoes and stockings.

The woman, a Miss Grabb, and Kate seemed to like each other and there was an offer of some work for two days a week, Friday and Saturday, though this would mean leaving Edward and Clara, but she had no choice. She was almost at the end of her tether as well as the end of town.

When she arrived home, Kate explained to the children about the work and that they would have to stay in bed where it was warm until it was light and on no account go wandering off. Kate knew the house would be cold for them but couldn't afford the money for coal. She couldn't ask the neighbours to look after them as they were in the same position and would expect a penny or two which she really couldn't spare. They were just about keeping their heads above water but no more, there was nothing left to pawn, she had darned and better darned clothes though Edward's were certainly getting too small and there wasn't much of a hem left on Clara's dress.

Each week she bought less and less food, especially meat, and the stew became weaker as the days went on. Bread was cheaper if it was stale, a day or two old, when they soaked it in thin gravy to fill them up. Kate couldn't remember the last time she had bought tea, making do with water.

All the walking to and from work had put a hole in the sole of her boot and no amount of stuffing it stopped her stocking becoming wet through while her feet became blue with cold, making it difficult to walk. If she could have laughed, she would have at the thought of how ironic, working in a shop selling shoes when her own were falling off her feet. She was relieved when the pewter skies turned into a lighter grey with clouds scudding along and it was such a day when she thought that the Gods were indeed looking down on her.

Feeling she had turned a corner, literally, two things sort of fell into her lap. The first was as she was cutting through the streets on her way to work that she saw a sign, in one of the small terraced house windows, saying it was up for rent. It was much smaller than the house they were in, Ted's house, but the rent reflected that in being almost half what she was paying. She knew she was paying a premium for being in the better part of town and having a third bedroom but she had to be realistic that sacrifices would have to be made if the three of them were to survive.

Kate arranged to view it with Edward and Clara in the hope that the move would not be too big a wrench for them. After all, the house they were in was the only one they had ever known. It was a basic two up two down, almost identical to the one her parents had lived in, though the rooms were smaller and it did not have a room in the attic. It did have a nice bay window to the front room, letting in plenty of light, not that it mattered too much as the houses opposite were quite close so she would have to put lace curtains against the window panes. The kitchen was basic with a sink, the cooker set into the chimney breast. The back door led to a yard which housed the outside toilet and coal house. Kate was pleased that the outside space wasn't shared. There was another door to the ginnel where the coal man would deliver his coal.

Kate agreed with the rent collector that she would move in the following Monday, showing him her rent book to prove she was a regular payer.

She talked to Edward and Clara about the move, explaining how it had been difficult to make ends meet since their father had died. She also went to the school to ensure they would both be able to remain there. It would be a longer walk for them but not so far for Kate to go to work. At school, Clara was always known as Clara Williams and over the years Kate had never put them wise that she was Stainbank, as they hadn't formally adopted her.

Things she didn't need for the move Kate quickly sold. There was no point in taking an extra bed and chairs as they wouldn't fit in anyway. She arranged for a man with a cart to move her belongings on the Monday as soon as the children had left for school. He had to do two runs, which cost more, but Kate just about managed. She bagged up what coal was left to take with her which was just as well as there was none in the new house.

On her way to collect Edward and Clara from school, she went by Ted's grave to talk to him about why she had to move. It saddened her that there was still no memorial plaque to say what had happened.

On the Friday of the same week as they moved, Kate was rushing home along Linthorpe Road. She would not normally have gone that way but cut through the streets. The mud was cloying and she wanted to walk along a better pavement to get home without getting her dress and coat covered. She saw a sign in the bakery window asking for a shop assistant. Before she had chance to think about it, she was in being interviewed by the baker. He wanted someone six days a week to work from eight till two while he was out delivering his goods. She didn't care about the hours, only the wages and hopefully this would keep the debtors from their door.

The baker seemed canny enough. He was a one man business but he needed help as the delivery service had taken off. He had thought about getting someone to take the cart out but he liked being out and about himself. Kate agreed to work on a trial basis to see how they got on. Although she was sad to leave the shoe shop, the walk wasn't so far. She did purchase a pair of discounted boots from Miss Grubb. One had been bleached a pale brown from being in the shop window too long, the other a dark brown but she thought she could stain them both black with coal dust and water.

As she lay in bed that night, she thought how things had changed. If she had seen the advert first, she may not have had to move house though she was happier that the bills were smaller. The children seemed happy enough and the neighbours were friendly. All in all, she was content though she still missed Ted terribly.

Each Saturday she would bring home what was left of the bread and currant buns which she shared with some of her neighbours when there was plenty to go round. It made her feel part of the community, something she hadn't realised she missed. She wasn't a snob but had never really needed the neighbours before when she had Ted and his mother, or her family close by and when they all went, she retreated into herself, caring only about Edward and Clara.

Edward found a job with the milk man, going out on the rounds before school which helped, and the pint of milk he brought home each day was shared. He looked a lot like his father though didn't have his singing voice nor his Welsh lilt. His accent was definitely Middlesbrough, whatever that was as it seemed a mix of many. The town was a melting pot from all over the country and world so had a definite dialect of its own.

Good old Queen Victoria had been on the throne sixty years in September 1896 but the celebrations for the diamond jubilee were not held until June of the following year when a national holiday was declared. Kate was pleased to hear the whole street was to hold a party, as were many others in the town. Luckily she wouldn't need to be too involved. She laughed when she heard a committee had been set up and she did only attend one meeting, due to work commitments she said.

It was agreed to charge threepence per child which could be paid to Mrs Thompson at number 10 over the weeks leading up to the party, to cover the cost of food. For the adults, anyone wanting anything other than tea would have to provide their own.

Kate was asked if she could get the bread at a reduced rate from the bakery to make sandwiches. Mr Taylor, the baker, said he could do better than that by making a miniature currant bun for each child. This was no mean feat as there were thirty-seven of them between the twenty houses.

Someone bought a box of plums to make jam from 'doggy' market, the local name for North Ormesby. Everyone referred to the area as 'doggy', though the reasoning differed. Some thought it was because men met there with whippets, or the smell from the glue factory smelt like wet animal fur. Even the idea that puppies had once been sold there. Kate didn't know the answer though everyone knew the area by that name.

The morning of the party began early with the men putting bunting across the street from the upstairs windows while the women swept the street before tables and chairs were put down the middle of the road for the children.

The ladies all wandered between houses to get the food prepared. Old widow Johnstone from number 3 had the big teapot so everyone supplied what tea they could spare. Edward had brought home extra milk, hopefully enough for each child to have a taste, leaving enough for tea. Kate sliced the bread in her kitchen while one of the neighbours put the jam on while another cut the bread into four to make bite sized sandwiches. Each plate would have a sandwich, a small currant bun and an apple.

Someone boiled a couple of dozen eggs which Kate mashed for adult sandwiches. She really enjoyed the camaraderie of the street, families mixing together, laughing and talking while the children were having the time of their lives.

Somehow, she wasn't sure how it happened but Kate was given a glass of sherry. It was far too sickly sweet, scrunching her face, and she decided she would rather to stick to tea. Once all the eating and drinking was over, the women washed up while the men and children returned the tables to the correct house. Then the games began, races up and down the street, while most of the women sat on chairs together, watching, drinking more tea or sherry and chatting.

Clara won a race and was awarded a homemade certificate and a gob stopper which kept her quiet for a long while though eventually she spit it into her handkerchief for later.

The afternoon spread into the evening with everyone still on the street, children playing marbles, the men and some women having a go at quoits while swigging beer. Kate knew it would soon start getting rowdy but she didn't want to be the first to leave. They wouldn't get much sleep anyway. Someone suggested they have a competition, one side of the road against the other. Kate was dragged to her feet to the cheering of Edward and Clara so she didn't want to be seen as a stick in the mud. To be truthful, Kate really enjoyed herself, finding she was quite good at quoits though it was probably more to do with the fact she was sober.

The evening darkened and the younger children were ready for their beds so Kate thought it would be a good time to say goodnight. Edward carried the kitchen chair as Kate put her arm round Clara's shoulder, all agreeing they had enjoyed the day.

It was strange, Kate thought, but she felt much happier in this house than Ted's, only because everyone looked out for each other. It wasn't the same as having family but the next best thing. All in all, for the first time in a long time, she felt settled.

Kate was surprised to receive a letter from Rachel to say she would visit for a few days on her way to Salisbury where she would be doing some nursing training before heading abroad with the Military Nursing Service. They hadn't kept in close contact over the years so Kate was looking forward to catching up. Edward readily gave up his bed for his auntie and both he and Clara were pleased to see her when she arrived with a large kit bag of gifts, socks, stockings, sweets, tea and a couple of books for Kate.

The whole house lightened as Rachel regaled them not only with her work but of creeping out of the nurses' home to go to parties with the doctors or porters. They listened, mouths open in amazement and for the first time in a long time, the house chimed with laughter. She talked of her work treating anything from a man with a pitchfork through his foot to amputations but pulled herself up short as she started talking about the men who were burnt. Quickly changing the subject, Rachel told them about the camaraderie of the soldiers on the wards. Rather than being cold dark places, they were full of fun when they all got together. Most were from the Durham Light Infantry and despite their terrible injuries, all seemed to look out for each other. It was because of them that she had decided to do her army nursing training, especially when they told her about the lack of equipment and nurses. She felt sorry for them. Some of the poor souls had died before receiving treatment and that wasn't right.

Edward asked if she had seen any bullets but she said no, only the effects they had on people. He wanted to know what the men said about the fighting but she looked at Kate who shook her head.

The following day when the children were still at school, Kate talked to Rachel about how difficult she was finding things. She hadn't realised what a struggle it would be. They talked about the family and Kate showed Rachel a letter from John.

"Do you ever wonder what really happened to Frank?" Rachel said, stopping Kate talking.

"What do you mean? He was murdered," she replied.

"Yes, but who did it?" Rachel replied.

"Oh, I don't know. The police thought it was one of his associates. I never heard anyone was charged. Why bring that up now?" Kate didn't know where this conversation was going.

"Do you remember when the police came round?" Rachel continued.

"Vaguely, it was a long time ago."

"Yes, well, I found our John in the ginnel, retching at the news. Why would it upset him so much? They were hardly close, were they?" Rachel was in her stride now.

"It affected us in different ways, didn't it? I mean, look at what happened to Alice and I wouldn't have Clara," Kate replied.

"Yes, but the two were linked, don't you think? Why was Frank killed the same night we found out about his involvement with Alice? Too much of a coincidence for me,"

Rachel stated. "I used to catch our mam and John talking but they would act dumb when they saw me."

"You're making things up, Rachel, just to fit a theory. You really cannot believe John had anything to do with it, surely not." Kate was incredulous.

"You weren't home, Kate. Our John had nightmares for months after. He started to stutter, didn't he?" Rachel continued.

"That was the shock. He was a sensitive boy," Kate replied.

"Why was mam so keen for him to emigrate then? Answer me that. She almost pushed him onto that boat to get away. I'm telling you, there was something odd about the whole thing." Rachel stood up. "Me throat's parched," she said, filling the kettle. "I'll tell you all I know then you tell me if I'm making it up." Rachel continued. "What happened to the bread knife then?"

"What are you talking about? Bread knife? You are talking in riddles, Rachel."

"You weren't living there but the night after Frank died, dad couldn't find the bread knife. Mam mumbled something, but it turned up later. And after that, well, you know John got married and emigrated as soon as he could."

"Alright, alright, I'll give you that but why are you bringing it all up now? Why don't you just leave it? Whatever happened happened. Don't rake it all up again," Kate said, sipping her tea.

"Well, and this is the funny thing. A man came into the hospital and saw my name and said he knew a Stainbank once who was from Middlesbrough. I pleaded ignorance but he told me the man had been murdered and at the time the rumour was he'd been done in by a rival gang but they always denied it." Rachel hardly seemed to pause for breath.

"They would, wouldn't they?" Kate replied.

"Well, no, that was odd, he said, no, they would have bragged about it to frighten off anyone wanting to move in and take over the 'business' whatever that was. He said, and these were his words not mine, 'They were sure it was personal but the police were too stupid to take it further'." Rachel let out a big sigh. "I just laughed at him and said I was glad it wasn't a relative of mine, and anyway I was from Stafford."

"I don't know what to say. I'm shocked, really I am. I can't believe it, not our John. So mam knew all about it at the time and never said anything. Do you think dad knew?" Kate asked.

"No, definitely not at the time but I don't know now. It's a hard secret to keep. I'm sorry, Kate. I had to talk to someone about it because it's been preying on my mind. I know it can't change anything." Rachel took Kate's hand. "I know we've never been close because our lives have been so different but perhaps now is a good time to change that."

"I'd like that. Even with the children, sometimes I feel so lonely." Kate stopped herself from crying. She was emotional over what Rachel had told her but also her own circumstances and it threatened to overwhelm her.

"Talking of families, does Clara know about her parentage?" Rachel asked.

"No, I know I should tell her but I can't find the right words. How can I explain how she came about. Everyone knows her as Clara Williams and anyway Alice has never bothered," Kate explained.

"Well, all I can say, and I'm sure you don't want my opinion, is the longer you leave it, the harder it will be," Rachel told her.

"I know, I know but she has always been my daughter. Ted loved her like his own. How on earth do I tell her?" Kate asked. "She's such a happy child, well, when she isn't in a mood. She does have a temper on her."

"You might end up regretting it if you don't," Rachel stated "Especially if someone else does."

"It's my decision and I'll have to live with the consequences," Kate replied. To change the subject she asked, "Have you ever thought of getting married?"

"Oh, I've had offers in my time, many of them wanting a carer not a wife, but to be honest I love what I do and couldn't give it up. So there's your answer. I've never been maternal so what would I marry for? I'll just remain, what did they used to say, oh yes, a spinster of the parish."

The mood lightened as they fell into each other, laughing.

All too soon, Rachel was leaving. She had been like a whirlwind in the house. She hugged Edward to her, telling him he was a handsome boy just like his father, and to watch out as the girls would be swooning in a few years' time. As she hugged Clara, they were surprised when she asked, "Do I look like my dad?"

Rachel looked at Kate before answering, "Well, you've certainly got his eyes but I think you're more of a Stainbank."

Kate was happy that they had met Rachel. They seemed to have warmed to each other. She put her arms round Edward and Clara's shoulders as they waved her off before rushing off to school and work. Her thoughts continued to be consumed with John and what he had done. He should have left it to the police. Perhaps that was it. He didn't trust them and thought Frank would get away and escape justice but it was a big price to pay. He'd rushed off to New Zealand. He said all those years ago when he was just a boy that he would one day have to kill his brother and he had. Her head was spinning with it all. It just goes to show you never really know what's going on in people, she mused.

CHAPTER 21

Time passed so quickly and soon a new century was upon them. The whole street had a party where they wandered in and out of each other's houses. Even the children were allowed to stay up to celebrate this momentous night. Men stood in the street, drinking and smoking, while women enjoyed the chatter. They had all dressed up. The sky was clear, thousands of stars out for the occasion as they waited for the Town Hall clock to strike midnight. The ships' hooters on the River Tees sounded and the men went first footing. It was the first time since Ted's demise that Kate could honestly say she had enjoyed herself and felt this would be a better year. The couple of shandies she had drunk helped. They all toasted good old Queen Victoria, Prime Minister Robert Gascoyne-Cecil, better known as the Marquess of Salisbury… anyone they could think of to raise a glass to.

She let Edward do the first footing through the front door to welcome in the New Year, out of the back to say goodbye to the old year. She hoped he would bring her luck but more importantly a contentment which her heart ached for. Everyone was late to bed, even the children, and no one before the early morning of the 1st January 1900. She was thankful they all slept long into the morning, and even then were loath to get out of their warm beds.

Life continued, Kate wouldn't have said happily, but accepting. Life went on through the spring, summer when Edward was fourteen and had already left school. He stood head and shoulders above her. He wasn't sure what he wanted to do, though there wasn't much work to be had. It was another year of depression. Men stood on street corners, hoping for an hour or two of work to keep the workhouse at bay. Kate didn't want him in the steelworks, thinking about his father, but nor did she want him on the river. It was a conundrum which seemed to have no answer as he continued to work with the milkman.

AFTER THE EXCITEMENT of the previous New Year, this one seemed a little flat. Yes, the street got together to welcome in the New Year but there was no money in many households. There was a depression in the town, a lot of people found themselves having to return to the mercy of their families to get by. Kate wondered what happened to Ted's friends. She hadn't kept in touch and the sound of their melodious voices broke her heart. She knew the choir was still going, winning many competitions but she couldn't ever go and listen. She had very briefly enjoyed the company of Mr Evans but hadn't contacted him when she moved, well, the truth was she didn't want to be a burden on him. It would never have worked. Every time she heard his voice all she could think of was Ted and even Mr Evans could never aspire to the pedestal she had placed her beloved husband on from the first moment she had met him.

In January 1901 Queen Victoria died and the country had a new king, Edward VII. The whole country was in mourning with flags at half mast on all buildings. Many people wore black in reverence to the old Queen, making the town seem darker, gloomier somehow. It seemed this time of year never saw the sun, smog permeated everywhere, people coughing as they went about their business.

Kate always got home to a cold house where her first job was to get a fire going before Clara returned from school and Edward got back from looking for work. She worried about them wearing damp clothes, remembering how ill her mam had been when she caught pneumonia. Coats, hats and scarves would be hung on the clothes horse in the living room to dry, steam coming off them.

She wouldn't say they were wealthy but they were certainly better off than some families who had no one in the household working, and if it wasn't for the free bread and milk each week they would be poorer for it.

One day, a letter arrived. Kate didn't recognise the handwriting. It was more a note really, from Alice. She informed her that their mother had died, followed three weeks later by their father. She, Alice, was selling what she could to try to cover the cost of the funerals before moving to become a housekeeper for the verger of her local church.

Kate looked at it. There was no forwarding address, no asking how they were, nor any mention of Clara. Looking at the single sheet of paper, she thought that in a way her parents had been lost to her the day they returned to the Midlands. Mam always had a weak chest after the pneumonia and dad had a dry hacking cough from the dust in the pottery. She didn't cry as she thought she would. At least they would be together.

She wondered if she should write straight back to Alice before she moved, but then again what would be the point? Instead, she would write a long letter to John and Ellen. They were her closest family, not in distance, but she always felt they were on her side. Life seemed to have many ups and downs and she supposed it was how people dealt with them which made them stronger. Life for the Williams family would go on, made better if Edward could find some kind of work.

However, things came to a head when she was suddenly dismissed from her job with the baker. Money had gone missing from the till though Kate knew she hadn't taken it. The only person other than the baker himself was his daughter who had been in to help package the bread to be delivered. Kate didn't know if she had been in the till, why would she, but Emily was the only one. Kate had tried to defend herself. "Why would I take money? I can manage now. If I was going to take anything, it would have been at the beginning when I was in financial difficulties. Why would I risk losing my job, I ask you?" she cried.

"Well, someone has taken the shilling and it's not me, so who else could it be? Answer me that if you can," he rounded on her.

"Ask your daughter. Have you taken it, Emily? Have you? Come on, be honest." Kate looked at the girl who shook her head but didn't look up.

"There's your answer, now take your coat and get out before I call the police. I'll sort out what you are due by Monday. Call in then." The baker turned his back on Kate.

"Please, Mister Taylor, I promise on my life I haven't taken any money from you. Talk to Emily and I'll come back Monday," Kate almost begged.

"You'll not accuse my daughter, now get away with you else I will call the police, I'm telling you."

Kate picked up her coat, showing the baker her pockets which were empty but to no avail. As she walked toward home, she was shaking. That little minx must have taken the money, she was certain, but why... that was the question she would like to know. Where would she get a job now without a reference? She had liked the job in the baker's because she was always home for Clara coming out of school, except the

Saturday when they both had to fend for themselves. She had always brought a spare loaf home, especially at the weekend so had managed to save a little bit of money but that would stop now.

Kate didn't think her Monday could get any worse but she was wrong. She waited until the afternoon to visit the baker's when she knew he would have finished his deliveries.

After an unsettled weekend worrying how things would turn out, she half expected Mr Taylor to apologise and tell her he had made a mistake. However Kate saw by the look on his face as she opened the bakery door it wouldn't happen.

He counted out what she was due, placing it on the counter top, saying, "I'm very disappointed it's ended like this. I trusted you, Mrs Williams."

"And so you should, Mr Taylor. I didn't take that money. You know deep down I didn't take it." She was tempted to give him the shilling but that would have made her guilty. She knew he wouldn't give her a reference but she continued, "I hope you won't blacken my name, Mr Taylor, else I'll have to go to the police myself and neither of us would want that."

The house was empty when she got home. Clara was still at school while Edward had gone off with some of his friends to find a job. He was still helping on the milk round but his wage and the pint of milk wouldn't keep them going for long. Picking up the Linthorpe Pottery vase, Kate fingered it carefully before tipping the coins onto the table. She thought of John and his family in New Zealand, wondering how they were. She often thought of him so far away, wondering if what Rachel had told her was true but she could hardly write and ask, could she?

Sometimes she thought she should have gone to her parents in the Midlands years ago but she knew why she hadn't… Clara. She was afraid Alice would claim her as her own if they were close by and what would happen then? Kate thought she might have been able to bear that if her second son had lived. He was born before Clara was a year old but then she would have another child to feed. Sighing, Kate thought there was no point becoming maudlin. It was what it was. She had made her choices, for better or worse.

Putting her money from the vase and her wages together, Kate calculated she had enough, if she was careful, to cover rent, paraffin, coal and food for six weeks, praying no one would become ill before she found another job. She smiled to herself… that was an awful thing to think. She didn't want anyone to fall ill at any time, even when she was working, though how she would manage without a reference she didn't know.

Clara got home first, bounding with energy. She never seemed still for a moment. Kate watched her animatedly telling her something that had happened at school, her bag on the table, coat thrown over a chair while her hair had long given up on the ribbons.

They were still chatting when Edward returned. He seemed almost as excited as Clara.

"You look happy," Kate said as he took a chair. "Have you found something?"

"Yes," Edward replied. "I've taken the King's shilling and joined the army." He placed the shilling on the table.

He was about to go on when there was a banshee scream which seemed to echo around the room. Kate realised it was coming from her. "You can't, you're not old enough. Tell me, is this some stupid joke?" She grabbed at her throat as though being choked but it didn't stop the noise coming out of her mouth. "You can't do this to me. There must be something you can do?" Large tears were falling down her face.

"We've been everywhere and couldn't get set on. Alf managed to get something on the docks 'cause his uncle's there." Edward had to shout to make himself heard. "The rest of us walked all along the Tees but even the small boat builders had nothing." Edward looked at Kate but she couldn't speak. "We walked to Dormanstown and Grangetown to the steelworks but they had already taken on for this year."

"Did you tell them who your dad was?" Kate sobbed. It sounded more like a death groan.

"Course I did but they told me they had nothing, so me, Joe, Thomas and Freddie saw the army man near the Town Hall. He called us over and said if we were sixteen he could offer us a job for life." Edward became excited. "We all told him we were, signed on the dotted line and he gave us all a shilling."

"Well, you're not going. I'm telling you that. You're still a boy, my boy, and I'm telling you now, you're not going. Are you listening to me, Edward. You're not fifteen for another five months," Kate shouted. "I'll come with you tomorrow and tell them. We can give them the shilling back. Yes, that's what we'll do, tell them it was a mistake."

"No, you won't, mam. The Sergeant Major said if we'd lied we would go to prison, anyway I want to join the army. We all agreed and now I've taken the shilling, it's a contract but it means I've got a job for life. He said we could nominate someone to get a share of my wages, so I've said you. You'll get a book to take to the post office each week so you won't have to worry about finding another job."

"Oh Edward, Edward, what have you done?" Kate hugged him to her. "What am I going to do without you." She could see the excitement in his face but her heart was breaking. "There must be something we can do? I'll soon find a job," she told him. "Haven't I always taken care of you?" Her chest was heaving as she spoke.

"I've got to be responsible, mam. I'm the man of the house and I should be supporting both of you so now I can. I'll get leave to come and see you both, just think I'll be going all round the country. I'll see places I've never even heard of." Edward was getting into his stride now.

"Just promise me you'll all stick together," Kate responded, still thinking she could go and find this Sergeant Major and give him a piece of her mind.

Later that night as she lay in bed trying to think what to do, Clara put her thoughts into words.

"Mam, will Edward have to fight, with a rifle and that?"

"No, no, I shouldn't think so. There's no fighting in this country," Kate replied unconvincingly.

A few days later, after not persuading Edward to change his mind, Kate and Clara walked with him to the railway station. The other boys all had the same bundles under their arms, as well as other mothers who were trying not to cry. Kate was surprised at the number waiting for the train. She walked up to one of the uniformed soldiers.

"Which one is the Sergeant Major?" she asked. "He signed these boys up under age."

"I know nowt about that, Mrs, and anyway he ain't here and we've got our orders. All these lads signed up to the army. No one forced them." He stood to attention. "Right, lads, those of you who took the King's shilling need to board the train. Say goodbye to your loved ones." He turned to the mothers. "I'll make sure your little darlings write. Those who can."

With that, the train doors slammed shut. The families watched as the train chugged out of the station. Kate couldn't speak. She knew she would make a fool of herself, wanting to fall to her knees and cry. Instead, she took Clara's arm and set off to walk out of the station, along Albert Road to Borough Road before turning right into Linthorpe Road and home.

Neither spoke when they got into the house. It seemed eerily quiet. Normally Edward and Clara would be vying for attention but the poor child was lost for words for the first time in her life, as was Kate.

"Come on, Clara, let's be happy for him," Kate said. "He was brave to make that choice. It will make a man of him. His dad would be very proud." She thought if only Ted were here, it would never have happened. He would have set him on at the steelworks and looked after him. She felt as though she had not only failed her son but her husband.

Both of them picked at their tea so Kate tipped it back into the pan. Waste not, want not. Is this what it was going to be like from now on, she wondered.

As they lay side by side in the double bed, they knew the other wasn't asleep but didn't want to break each other's thoughts, so they just lay there, side by side as darkness enfolded them.

For the next few days and weeks, Kate kept herself busy by walking around the town looking for work. Some seemed interested until she told them she had no reference from her previous employment. She explained time and again that she hadn't taken the money but it was the same response, thanks but no thanks. She had received the pay book from the army which was to pay her four shilling a week, not quite a fortune but enough to keep the wolf from the door in the short term.

They both found their own way to miss Edward and somehow life got into the same routine. Her heart ached as though he was lost to her just like his father. She remembered someone once said to her that no good comes of grieving for what you have already lost. She didn't understand it at the time but did now. Edward had made his decision for her and she should be grateful to him. She would pray for him to keep safe because he was a good boy, a credit to her.

Kate would watch Clara set off for school before gathering up the breakfast pots to be washed later in the day. Her plan was to try the factories which had sprung up around the river though she didn't know what kind of work would be open to her. Her mind went back to when Rachel was looking for work. She had placed a card in the post office window so Kate set about writing something. It couldn't hurt.

Position Wanted
Mature lady looking for employment
Experience of working in a factory (Linthorpe Pottery)
Shop work and running her own home and bringing up children.
Full or part time, to live out.
Anything legal considered. Wages negotiable.

She didn't know what else to write but didn't want it to be too long and detailed but enough to spread it out for any number of positions. More information would come later if she got an interview.

CHAPTER 22

Life became mundane for Kate. She was tired of being turned down for everything. She had skills, surely her luck would change soon. Her day brightened when she finally received a letter from Edward. It seemed he was having the time of his life. Inside was a sepia photograph taken when he passed his basic training and put on his uniform. Although he looked serious, his eyes had the mischief of his father. He seemed so grown up, even his writing seemed much more mature. She worried about him heading off to Portsmouth… that could only mean he was heading abroad.

By the time she got to the end of the letter, tears were streaming down her face. Her boy, her son, was now a man and she rejoiced that he seemed happy enough. At least he was with his friends and she was sure they would look out for each other.

Clara read and re-read the letter, talking all the time about what Edward was doing and asking where they thought he would be now.

They were both happy, especially Kate, to know Edward was safe and well. Standing the photograph against the vase, she could touch them together in the hope it would bring him luck. She thought of Edward and John at the same time.

Kate's mood lightened after receiving the letter though her finances did not. She was grateful for the four shilling a week she received from Edward but it wasn't enough. In desperation, she walked to the bottom of Linthorpe Road to see if Miss Grabb at the Shoe Emporium had any hours she could give her. Her old employer welcomed her warmly but couldn't help as she had taken on a young girl to train. Kate told her the story of how she had ended up with no reference. Miss Grabb offered to write one for her so all was not lost.

Armed with the reference, Kate tried the Grand Hotel opposite the railway station but no luck. She next tried the King's Head Hotel on the corner of Newport Road. It seemed it was a regular venue for all sorts of social clubs but it also had a licensed restaurant. She was fortunate, the manager told her, one of the waitresses had left. The hours would be part time Friday and Saturday from four until nine or ten, depending on when the last meal was served.

The hours were terrible for Kate. She would have to leave Clara alone but accepted gratefully. They would provide her with an apron and cap but she would have to wash them herself. The wages still wouldn't be enough to make the two of them comfortable but it was a start. Buoyed with more confidence than she had felt for a few months, Kate called into the post office to see if anyone had left a message about the card she had placed in the window.

Edward's letter seemed to have brought her luck. Someone from the big houses on the Avenue in Linthorpe were looking for a daily. Kate took the card, going straight to the house to enquire, hoping the job hadn't already been taken. She was shown into the drawing room, the front room, where a Mrs Brent told her she had had a couple of live in staff, usually taking on young girls to train in domestic duties but they didn't stay long.

Kate wondered why but after a brief discussion, Mrs Brent told Kate the hours were eight until three Monday to Friday and she should report to the cook the following day. Again, the money wasn't brilliant and the Friday she would have to go from one job to the other but it was something. She would need to talk to Clara about looking after herself but she was old enough now, almost ready for leaving school and finding work herself which would ease Kate's burden.

Kate found it hard doing the two jobs. To be truthful, she preferred the waitressing at the King's Head Hotel though she was on her feet all the time. Customers and staff seemed pleasant enough, and the tips which were shared out nightly were an added bonus. If she didn't finish until later, she would get the tram, just a couple of stops, with one of the other waitresses.

Working for Mrs Brent was another matter altogether and certainly for the first few weeks Kate had to bite her tongue. First it had been the scrubbing of the steps. According to Mrs Brent, she had used too much soap. People would slip so they had to be scrubbed several times in clean water. Kate knew it wasn't true. The piece of carbolic would hardly have given enough of a lather to wash your hands. Then there had been the incident of the black leading of the fireplace. Kate had cleaned both fireplaces, one in the lounge, the other in the dining room. She heard someone open the door and knew who it would be so carried on, using a shoe brush to put on the polish.

"You're putting too much on," Mrs Brent shouted. "What is it with you people, do you think I've a never ending pot of money?" When Kate didn't answer, she demanded, "Well, do you?"

Kate wanted to say who do you mean by you people, you're a nobody, you think you're better than you are. But she didn't. Instead she replied, "I'm sorry, Mrs Brent," as contritely as she could.

"More elbow grease, that's what's needed, now get a move on." With that, she went out of the front door to one of her 'charity events'.

Once she was sure Mrs Brent wouldn't return, Kate finished what she was doing, taking everything through to the kitchen and placing it on the floor of the broom cupboard. Washing her hands, Kate looked at Muriel the cook, and Aggie the maid. They lived in a room in the eves of the house. They were like mother and daughter though Aggie had been left in the workhouse as a baby.

"What's up with her majesty today? She's worse than usual," Kate asked.

"The master didn't come home last night," Aggie stated. "Third time this week. He'll have a new lady friend."

"What do you mean?" Kate asked, taking a cup of tea from Muriel.

"Oh, come on, Kate, you've been married so you know what men are like." Muriel laughed.

"My Ted wasn't like that." Kate was shocked at the thought.

"Well, if they can't get it at home they'll go elsewhere. It's nature," Muriel stated as Aggie nodded as though she knew all about it. "Here's Joe. Ask him about it."

Kate blushed as Joe asked, "What's nature?" Joe lived with his widowed mother and sister and from what Aggie said they were all a bit slow but he did wonders with the garden. He nurtured anything and they grew big and bold in thanks. His domain was the greenhouse where he was forever planting seeds, potting or sitting on an old stool, smoking his pipe.

Fortunately Kate didn't have to respond as Muriel

buttered scones for each of them. "Here, Joe, take these home." She gave him three warm scones wrapped in a napkin. "Don't forget to bring it back else she'll have me guts for garters. Here, Kate, there's a couple for you and your girl."

"Thanks, Muriel, but I don't want you to get into trouble," Kate replied.

"Oh, don't worry, the Mrs knows nowt about what I spend the housekeeping on. She thinks 'cause I can't read and write I can't add up. Me and Aggie will soon have enough to run away to London." Muriel laughed at Kate's face. "Don't be daft, lass. I've never been further than Newport Road corner."

"Well, next time you both have a day off, how about us getting the tram to Redcar. We could have a paddle in the sea," Kate replied, feeling sorry for the pair of them, though the truth was she had only been the once.

"Could me mam and sister come?" Joe asked, his moon face shining.

"Anyone can come," Kate said, wondering how this would ever work but got up to carry on with her chores or she would be late getting home.

As Kate buttered the scones for supper later that evening, she remembered the conversation. "Can you remember when we all went on a trip to Redcar?"

"Yes, it was such fun, but I was only small then. Why?" Clara asked, savouring the scone.

"Muriel, Aggie and Joe have never been and I sort of promised we would all go when they get a day off." Kate sighed. "Why don't we go one Sunday? We could take sandwiches… better still fish and chips."

"Can we, mam? It would be lovely to have a day out, something to write to Edward about." Clara's face lit up.

"I wonder where he is. It's been months since he wrote. I miss him, Clara."

"I do as well, my annoying big brother. Do you think I could move into his room?"

"Of course, lass. I didn't want to push you out of my bed but you do keep me awake with your snoring." Kate laughed and they hugged each other.

For the next few months, Kate watched the diners at the hotel more closely, wondering who was with their wives and who was with their lady friends. She came to the conclusion that the more dowdy and downtrodden the woman looked, the little conversation between the two, she was probably the wife. Those who made an effort, brighter make up and conversation was probably the lady friend.

She made up stories about them in her mind. She also wondered if any of them were Mr Brent. She had never met him. He had always left the house before she arrived.

That was until she had been at the Avenue for six months. She arrived to find both Muriel and Aggie in the kitchen. Without a good morning, Aggie piped up, "All hell broke loose last night and this morning. She's screaming at him like a fish wife, the language, I've heard nothing like it."

"What's happened?" Kate said when she could get a word in.

"Dunno but I'm keeping out the way," Aggie stated.

"I've no time for that, I need to get on. I need to be away right on three. Where are they?" Kate asked.

"In her bedroom. She's flinging things about." Aggie nodded.

Putting on her apron, Kate picked up the bucket to clean the floors and set off through the door. She didn't get far, colliding with Mr Brent as he hurried down the stairs. As the bucket fell, Kate put her hands out to stop being thrown to the ground. Water flowed over the tiles toward the rug which she ran to pick up.

"Get out of my way," Mr Brent said, trying to push her to one side.

"Don't you push me, I'm trying to save your expensive rug," she replied, looking at him for the first time.

"You? What are you doing here?" he said, looming over her.

"I work here, I'm the daily." Kate stood tall, keeping eye contact.

"You work at the King's Head Hotel?" he stated, though it was more of a question.

"Yes, I do. I don't think it's against the law to have two jobs." Kate didn't want to feel subservient.

"It all makes sense now. Someone has been tittle tattling to my wife." Mr Brent stabbed a finger at her.

"I hope you are not referring to me. I don't know what you are talking about. I've seen you in the restaurant but didn't know you were Mr Brent until now."

"Let me make it clear. I won't have people gossiping, do you understand? Now get out of my house. From now on you are no longer in my employ."

Kate was about to speak but placed the rug on the stair, picked up the bucket and mop, passing the latter to Mr Brent. "You had better get mopping then. Can I just say, I'm not the one who has spoken to your wife so you need to look elsewhere for the gossip." She was about to leave but turned back. "I'm sure Mrs Brent will be pleased to be undermined in her own home. I'll leave it to you to tell her you've sacked me." With that she went to the kitchen where Muriel and Aggie were agog.

"What on earth have you done?" Muriel asked. "Speaking to him like that."

"I've told the truth, Mu. He's been in the King's Head with a lady but I didn't know it was him. I'm not going to be blamed for his misdemeanours." Kate took off her apron and cap. They heard the front door slam. "Sorry, Aggie, you'd better go and clean up the mess."

She was sorting out her basket which was being filled with food by Muriel when Aggie returned.

"The Mrs wants to see you in the dining room."

Kate knocked quietly before entering. Mrs Brent was standing by the window. In that moment she felt sorry for her. "You wanted to see me?"

"Yes, yes, I heard your conversation. Is it true you've seen him with his mistress?" She spat the word.

"I have seen him dining there but I didn't know it was him and that's the truth." Kate told her. "I'm sorry, Mrs Brent. I'm not a gossip but your husband has blamed me and sacked me but I'm hoping you would give me a reference." Kate was about to go on but was interrupted.

"No, that won't do. I'm in charge of this house and I'm not sacking you."

"Thank you, Mrs Brent." Kate was surprised but understood.

"Oh, you might not thank me when I tell you what I want you to do, and this is strictly between you and I, understand?"

Kate nodded, not really understanding at all but at least her job was saved.

"I want you to tell me when you see my husband and look closely at his paramour so you can describe her to me."

"Paramour?" Kate repeated.

"His woman, his mistress, whatever you want to call her," Mrs Brent snapped.

"I'm not happy about getting involved but will do this for you once and once only," Kate told her. "Will that be all?"

This time it was Mrs Brent who nodded before turning back to the window, dismissing Kate. When she returned to the kitchen, Muriel had packed food into Kate's basket. "What's this?" she asked.

"To help you," Muriel responded.

"I'm not going anywhere. Mrs Brent has accepted my account of things so I'm stopping." Kate picked up her apron and went back to her cleaning.

Muriel and Aggie looked at one another. Something's going on, they both said in their own way.

Fortunately for Kate, she didn't see Mr Brent and his paramour, as his wife had called his mistress. Paramour... she liked the word, though not its meaning. She assumed he was giving the hotel a wide berth until the trouble died down at home. Kate reported to Mrs Brent that there was actually nothing to report. She tried to remember what the paramour had looked like but was vague. The truth was she couldn't remember and hoped it would be the end of the matter and her life could continue as before.

However, it was taken out of her hands when she arrived for work at the hotel the following week. The manager called her into his office. "We have had a complaint about your attitude toward customers and I can't have that." He was about to go on when Kate interrupted.

"Is that one complaint by one person or by a number of people?" she asked.

"Well, it's a number by one person who has implied that you were rude to him and his guest," he replied.

"That will be a Mr Brent, I assume. I don't suppose he gave you the full account of why he sees fit to make a complaint about me. I haven't been rude to him or anyone for that matter." Kate was angry.

"I'm not at liberty to disclose but you understand we take any complaints very seriously." The manager shifted in his chair.

"If it is Mr Brent, I'll tell you why he has done this, shall I?" Kate didn't wait for a reply. "He has been to this restaurant, wining and dining his paramour." She saw the look on the manager's face. "His mistress. His wife found out and he's blaming me but I didn't say anything. It's not my place."

"How do you know his wife?" the manager asked, realising he'd given the complainant away.

"I work for her as a daily. He saw me at the house and put two and two together but made five, I'm afraid, because I didn't know who he was until then," Kate replied.

"Well, that's as may be, Mrs Williams, but he is a regular patron of ours and has some standing in the community," he told her.

"Oh, I see, and I'm just one of the small people trying to make a life for me and my family and you don't have the backbone to believe what I'm telling you. The truth will out. It's funny how you turn a blind eye to the philandering that goes on in this hotel but you don't believe an honest person like me." Kate drew breath.

The manager had nothing to say so stood up, going to the cabinet for the petty cash and took out a florin. "I'm sorry, Mrs Williams, but I have to take this seriously."

"You're going to sack me for one complaint so you are not sorry enough. I hope you're happy, pushing my family toward the workhouse. How does that make you feel?" Kate picked up the florin and flung her apron and cap onto the desk before walking, her back straight, toward the main entrance of the hotel.

CHAPTER 23

Kate read and re-read the letter, not taking in what it said. It informed her that her son, her beautiful boy Edward, had been killed in a skirmish in South Africa. He would be greatly missed by his comrades. The letter continued, "You have the consolation of knowing that he died for King and country which is the highest honour a soldier can have. He is buried in a military cemetery near Ladysmith in South Africa."

Kate grabbed at the back of a chair, the groan coming from the pit of her stomach until she screamed, gripping her arms tightly round herself. This could not be happening. He was just a boy, her boy. It seemed he had been in the army just over a year and she thought wars were over. No one talked about them so what had happened for him to die like that, in a foreign land. She would never find comfort at his grave.

Clara found her distraught, her chest heaving with sobbing. The pain imploded again as Clara joined in. Their bodies rocked in grief as they held each other tightly. When they could cry no more, they climbed under the eiderdown on the bed, getting warmth from each other until they fell asleep, both dreaming of Edward, a most wonderful son and brother who had given his life for them.

Kate was relieved that it was the weekend where she could remain in the house with the curtains closed in memory of Edward though he had died months ago. Her face was drawn, eyes puffy from crying. She knew she looked a mess if she looked as bad as Clara.

Was she a bad person to be relieved that she wouldn't have to find the money for a funeral or burial plot? Her poor Edward would have been laid to rest in a shared grave no better than the workhouse. At least his grave was in the sun where he would feel the warmth. Oh! She was going mad. He would feel nothing and she had lost him the day he joined the army.

Both her and Clara had so much they wanted to say but couldn't such was the misery and physical pain they each felt. She allowed them to both wallow in their grief for most of the day but realised she had to pull herself out of her agony for the sake of her daughter.

Life went from bad to worse when a few days after her sacking from the hotel and worse after Edward's death, Kate slipped in the yard, badly twisting her knee. She could hardly walk which meant she couldn't get to her job with Mrs Brent.

"Listen to me, Clara," Kate said, "you'll have to go in my place for a week or so. Explain to Mrs Brent that I'll be back as soon as I'm on my feet."

Clara nodded, not keen to do domestic work even in the house. Since leaving school she had found no work. The town was still in a depression and with no experience it was even more difficult.

"Muriel and Aggie will help you. Are you listening to me, Clara?"

The girl nodded again.

"Don't answer Mrs Brent back with your cheek."

"Oh, I wondered when that would come up. It's not cheek, as you call it, I'm just standing up for myself," Clara snapped.

"Yes and it will get you nowhere, so think on," Kate told her.

Monday morning came and Clara went off with a number of instructions from Kate which put her in more of a mood. She hated it and lasted only three days before returning to the house, flinging her hat and gloves down on the table.

"She's a witch, that woman," Clara bemoaned. "Everywhere I went, she was behind me, telling me how to do this and that, so I told her if she was such an expert she could do it herself. She told me to tell you not to bother trying to beg for your job back. She doesn't want to see you."

"That's great, Clara, how are we going to pay the rent and get food? Answer me that!" Kate was almost shouting. "Do you think I enjoy being put upon day after day, cleaning up someone else's mess. Well, don't sit yourself down, my lady. Get yourself off and find a job, otherwise there will be no tea tonight."

Clara put her hat and gloves back on, marching out of the door which she slammed as Kate shook her head. What was she going to do with her? She had always been quick tempered but Kate put it down to being small… she needed to make herself heard. Well, she would see what it was like in the real world now.

By the end of the week, Kate was running out of money and Clara was no help so she made the decision to move into something smaller. She would be sad to leave the house as she had got on well with the neighbours but needs must and she wasn't the only person in this position. Using the walking stick she had been loaned, the two of them walked further into town toward the docks where the houses had been split into rooms. It wasn't the most salubrious of areas and many of the rooms were rented out to single men but the rent was much cheaper.

They managed to find a ground floor room which was filthy but Kate said she would take it the following week and paid two weeks rent up front. Now all she hoped was that she could get out of the other house before the rent man came knocking. Kate sorted through what she could take, the double bed being sold along with the bedding. The room would only hold a single bed, the two seater sofa and a side table with two chairs. She packed the kitchen utensils into a box. The kitchen table and two chairs she gave to one of the neighbours as payment in return for him using his hand cart to take her meagre belongings to the room.

Kate wanted to cry at what had become of her but couldn't let Clara see how bad she felt. They scrubbed the room with cold water from the outside tap. They had the luxury of a fireplace but no coal. The outside toilet was shared with the four rooms as was the kitchen but they had nothing to cook.

The following day Clara set off to look for work while Kate tried to make the best of the situation she was in. The neighbours were keen to introduce themselves. There was a family with three children on the first floor, a couple in what would have been the dining room and a single man in what would have been the small bedroom. Apparently, he worked nights at the docks so no one saw much of him. They all seemed dirty. She was sure they would have lice or nits so kept well clear.

Finally, Clara managed to find a situation through one of her old schoolfriends. It was in one of the big houses just out of town. She was to live in Monday to Saturday lunchtime but could come home for the rest of the day and the Sunday. It wasn't really what Kate wanted, she didn't want to be on her own, but had no choice. She promised once she found work they would move into better accommodation. Life got into a routine with Kate applying for any work going, a couple of hours cleaning, shop work, anything but she had no luck. She was lonely through the week, but happy that at least Clara was getting her meals.

Each Saturday Clara would turn up with the two shilling she had earned. Kate felt bad that she couldn't give the girl anything but she was still living hand to mouth. Once the rent was paid, she had no money for coal or tea, so never had anything warm inside her. Her dress was hanging off her bones, skin dry, scalp itchy. She had washed her hair under the outside tap with a sliver of carbolic. It looked dull, as dull as her eyes.

She loved Clara breezing in, full of stories of what had happened through the week. They laughed more but she always felt Clara was embarrassed by where they were living. They had to share the single bed on the Saturday night. Kate loved the feeling of warmth from her daughter. Clara on the other hand seemed to try and push herself as far away as possible.

Life wasn't perfect but they were muddling through as best they could. Kate hoped that things would look up soon. If only she could find herself a job for a few hours, it would help but everyone was tightening their belts.

Kate looked at the weak sun bringing shadows to the small room through the curtains which didn't quite meet at the window. This was her life now, existing in shadows, since the life she once knew had imploded. First on the death of her husband and then the demise of her boy, Edward.

She involuntarily shivered at the thought of her son lost in a war they knew nothing about. The black rimmed letter sat on the mantlepiece as though throwing it away would be the final insult to her son. He had sent her money from his pay regularly until his end. She thought how he had joined the army to help her and Clara. Now all she had to remind her that Edward had lived was her memories, the letter and a sepia photograph of him standing uncomfortably in his army uniform. He looked so young, just like his father with the dimple on his cheek, and although he was serious, his eyes smiled just for her. She didn't mourn him like she had his father though the loss was still hard to bear, perhaps because she had no body, no funeral. To be truthful, she had mourned him the day he got on the train at Middlesbrough Station. Now he was buried on a battlefield in southern Africa after fighting the natives.

After days of inclement weather, being stuck inside this one room, she needed a little fresh air. That was certainly true. There would be little fresh air wherever she went but she had to get out of this room before she went insane. The single bed took up most of the space on one wall as did the sofa next to the unlit fire. She tried to keep the place clean, sweeping flies both dead and alive from the window sill and picture rail but no amount of scrubbing could remove the stench from the sewers and smoke from the works. To bring a lightness to the room, several of her drawings adorned the walls, reminding her of her days at the Linthorpe Pottery which seemed a lifetime ago to her now.

Thinking of the pictures, she picked up her paper and pencils before taking them with a dining chair to a position by the wall in the yard. Ted had bought her the artist's pad years ago after the stillbirth of their second son. She involuntarily twisted her wedding ring, which was loose now, around her finger. Round and round, looking at the richness of the gold which shone like Ted's baritone voice, a sound she could hardly recall.

When she thought of her husband, her heart ached. There was always an empty space beside her where he should have been and no matter how long since his demise, the feeling never lessened. She hated living in the pungent room with a shared outhouse in a rat infested yard. Kate didn't fit in with the other families. They thought she was a little eccentric, drawing pictures no one round these parts could afford to buy. Drawing was the only thing that stopped her mind from screaming at the injustice her life had become.

The only ray of sunshine in her life now was Clara, who would be home again on Saturday afternoon. Like a whirlwind, she would breeze in full of herself. As if her thoughts brought forward an apparition, the girl marched through the back gate almost taking it off its hinges, her face like thunder.

"What on earth are you doing here?" Kate looked at this young woman who still looked in many ways like a child. Clara had always been small for her age, petite even, but she had a fierce temper and a determination which made up for her lack of stature.

"Nice to see you too, mam. I'm not talking about it out here." Clara marched into the one room through the kitchen. Her nose wrinkled at the stale smell of cabbage, and unmentionables.

"Have you been finished from your job again, Clara? You know this can't go on and you won't get a reference again." Kate sat on the sofa.

"Oh yes, blame me. You know nothing till I tell you, if you'll let me speak." Clara made a big thing about removing her gloves and hat before flinging them on top of her small bag.

"I'm waiting." Kate stared at Clara.

"Maybe I should ask you a question first?" Clara pulled out a chair but didn't immediately sit down.

"Oh, come on, don't be so dramatic. Just tell me what happened to make them sack you?" Kate sighed.

Shutting the door, Clara stood in front of her mam. "I'd rather the neighbours didn't hear this and I hope you'll find it in you to answer me honestly. Do you think it's right people call me names? Men think they can treat me with disdain because of who I am," Clara rasped.

Kate was about to speak but Clara put her hand up to silence her.

"Over the years I've heard whisperings and ignored them but now, today was the final straw. Mr Wrightson, the butler, said I didn't know my parentage. What does that mean? You owe me an explanation, mam," Clara sobbed.

Kate knew this day would come, of course she did. Should have had this discussion years ago but couldn't bring herself to do it, nor could she find the right words. As time went on it had became more and more difficult but she owed Clara the truth now she was no longer a child.

Taking a deep breath, Kate replied, "What do you want to know? I promise to be as truthful as I can."

"Ted Williams wasn't my real dad, was he?" Clara almost shouted.

Tears filled Kate's eyes as she began. "In every way Ted was your father. He loved you as much if not more than Edward. You gave your first smile to him and he loved you as his daughter. He worked hard to provide for his family and he would have been very proud of you, Clara. But no, you are right. He isn't your father in the sense he begat you but it didn't matter to him."

"Well, it matters to me because people are whispering and it hurts so I'm asking you who my father is?" Clara pulled her hand away from Kate.

"I honestly don't know who your father is. I don't know his name other than he was supposed to be a gentleman who once lived in one of the big houses."

"Did he attack you?" Clara asked, shocked.

"No, nothing like that. I really don't want to go through this, Clara."

"So you went willingly with him when you were married to Ted?"

The slap across her cheek shocked both of them.

"I'm sorry, Clara. I'm sorry I hit you. Can you forgive me?

Just know we both loved you, love you, and that's all that matters." Kate tried to take Clara's hands but was pushed away.

"This doesn't make sense." Clara put her hand to her cheek which was now smarting. "There's something you're not telling me. If this man didn't force himself on you and you didn't go willingly, then what?" Clara glared at Kate.

Kate couldn't answer. What could she tell her that would make the situation better?

"Maybe this will help you to tell me the truth," Clara snapped. "The footman called me a bastard. No one would want to marry me because I'm a bastard, that's what he said. I was sacked for slapping him hard. So come on!" Clara was about to explode.

Kate cried, cried for her child who had been treated so badly, crying for herself because she was a coward. She should have explained years ago.

"If you won't tell me everything, I'm leaving and I won't come back." Clara picked up her bag and gloves.

Kate took a deep breath which made her shudder. "Listen to me, Clara, and I'm telling you this because I love you and can see how much you are hurting. We both love you but Ted wasn't your dad and I'm so sorry I didn't explain before, but I'm not your mam."

Clara collapsed back onto the chair while Kate cried, attempting to breathe at the same time but huge tears rolled down her face. Neither spoke for what seemed like an eternity, Clara trying to take in what had been said to her. Kate didn't want to say any more but knew she had to put her daughter, the child she had brought up as her own, out of her misery.

"Your Auntie Alice was thirteen when she had you and she couldn't cope so we took you in. We so badly wanted you to be ours." Kate tried to smile at Clara but she continued to look down at her hands in her lap. "When they moved back to Stafford, the family agreed that you would be better with us and that was how it was. I should have told you before but I didn't ever want to admit that you weren't my baby."

"Shut up, just shut up. You're lying. You had a relationship with another man and now you are trying to feel better about it. I hate you," Clara screamed.

"Listen, Clara, the only thing I am guilty of is loving you like my own. I know it was wrong not explaining to you before but I could never find the right words or admit to myself that I didn't give birth to you. I love you and always will." Kate reached out to this complicated girl but Clara brushed her away.

"You have lied to me all my life. I'm not who I thought I was and neither are you. You are nothing to me, do you hear me? Nothing." She spat the word out before getting up from the chair.

Kate tried to hold her but she was pushed backwards where she landed on the bed. The look on Clara's face told her everything. The best thing was to stay quiet. She had to think this out for herself and let her take in what she now knew. "I'm sorry I didn't tell you before but I will never be sorry for loving you as my own, my daughter," Kate said, almost to herself as she watched Clara go out of the room.

CHAPTER 24

Kate didn't know how long she sat in the same position, weeping quietly, but the shadows of the late morning were now long gone and she shivered. Pacing up and down the small space, four steps one way and four steps back, she worried about what to do next. When would Clara be back? Where would she go? It was her fault this had happened but it didn't make her feel better to know that. She had been too wrapped up in her own grief to think how Clara would feel if she found out about her parentage from someone else.

The late afternoon turned into early evening and Kate became worried about the child, who really was a young woman but she shouldn't be wandering the streets alone. She didn't know if she should go out and look for her but what if Clara returned and she wasn't here. Her head ached with everything running around but she was sure she wouldn't feel half as bad as Clara at this moment. Kate didn't draw the curtains but sat looking out of the window at everyone who walked past, men returning from work, women going to buy a penny worth of beer to have with the evening meal, but no Clara.

Kate began to shiver as the evening wore on and she got into bed with the eiderdown around her shoulders where she sat waiting, just waiting. Every sound, every creak of the staircase made her look to the door, waiting for Clara. At some point she must have slept as she woke with a start when she heard the men's boots pounding the pavement on their way to work and rattle of milk bottles on the cart. Clara had been out all night. Kate didn't know any of her friends or where she could have gone but made a decision… if she didn't return by midday, she would have to go to the police station to report her missing. Kate didn't want to have to explain why they had argued but she had to find her, she just had to.

In the end she could wait no longer. Putting a brush through her hair, she put on her shabby coat before venturing out into the street. Slipping through the side streets, she looked up and down for any glimpse of Clara but her feet took her onto Linthorpe Road which was the main thoroughfare into town. As she stood watching people go about their business, horses and carts, cabs and all manner of humanity seemed to be about but no Clara.

What did she expect? Did she really think she would just arrive in front of her like yesterday, like an apparition? Kate's dilemma was should she continue into town and toward the police station or go up to the village where they had once lived? Maybe she had stayed with a neighbour. The centre of town was closer, shops would be opening and perhaps Clara would be wandering around, looking through the windows.

As Kate neared the small park next to the Town Hall, she saw a crowd gathering and was swept along with them. Men and women stood in a semi circle around a lady who was standing precariously on a wooden box, other women holding banners behind her on the Town Hall steps. She was calling, asking women to join in their fight for equality but Kate couldn't hear all what she was saying. Someone said it was Lord Bellamy's daughter so what did she know about suffering?

Men were laughing and heckling the women but the lady on the box continued with her argument. Kate asked the man next to her what was going on. He laughed, saying they wanted rights for women when the working man didn't have any so it would never happen. He laughed even louder as someone threw a stone, shouting, "Get home to yer man, he'll be expecting a meal on the table." A group of men joined in, picking up what they could find to throw at the women.

Kate tried to get closer in an attempt to listen but was jostled when a man grabbed the woman next to her, telling her to get away home. She was busy watching the couple arguing, the woman giving as good as she got. Kate thought the poor woman would probably end up with a black eye. She almost missed the kerfuffle on the steps as the police arrived, pushing the woman unceremoniously off the crate she had been standing on, much to the cheering of the crowd. The other women tried to help her up, and in all the fracas a policeman's hat was knocked off. Another tripped so he fell, to more cheering.

Kate realised Clara was in amongst it all. She tried to push her way through but was held back. Calling out made no difference in all the noise and all she could do was watch as the women were put in the Black Maria. Setting off at a run, Kate bumped and pushed into people, almost causing her own riot, as she tried to keep up with the horses. By the time she had apologised, the police had turned down the street into the back entrance of the Town Hall and into the police station.

Trying to speak to the desk sergeant, he told her that she could do nothing until the women had been processed so she would have to wait outside. Pacing up and down, Kate was frantic at what Clara had got herself into. She was biting the skin on her thumb as she felt the first drops of rain. By the time she was allowed into the police station, she was soaked. Water dripped off her hair, a puddle forming round her feet. She looked dishevelled as well as sounding pathetic as she asked about her daughter.

The desk sergeant was sympathetic but was insistent that Kate couldn't see Clara. She would be up before the magistrate the following day. If it was her first offence, she would be given a fine which would have to be paid before she could be released so to come back tomorrow.

Heading back to her room – Kate could never think of the place as home – she worried where she would get the money to pay Clara's fine. She had nothing of value anymore, it had all been sold in vain to try and keep the house she had lived in with Ted. All she had was the small Linthorpe Pottery vase on the mantlepiece, but had always promised her brother John who had the other one, that one day they would be reunited. How much it would be worth Kate didn't know but it was all she had.

She hadn't eaten today or yesterday, but all she had in the house was the crust of stale loaf, so realising how hungry she was, she cut it thinly before dipping it in the mug of water to soften it. It tasted awful, crumbs of the bread floated in the cold water, but Kate persevered. She had nothing else.

She was up the following morning as soon as the sun rose, reaching the pawnbroker to find a queue of women already waiting for the shop to open. She asked if she could do her business first. It was urgent, she told them. It's all urgent, Mrs, otherwise we wouldn't be here, came their reply. One needed money for the doctor as her children had croup, while another wanted to reclaim her husband's workboots because he had a couple of days work at the docks.

She moved back in line. She didn't want to admit she needed money to pay her daughter's fine. It seemed petty compared to other people's lives. She couldn't ever remember living this hand to mouth existence before, even as a child and she had looked down on those who did, never thinking that but for the grace of God. Now she was in that position, she could see how easily it happened with men out of work, several children to feed. Many of them including her had little to pawn but someone was still making plenty of money. She would have to stop grieving for those she had lost and find herself a job but first she had to save Clara.

When it was finally her turn, Kate placed the vase on the counter where the pawnbroker offered her two shilling for it. No, she told him it would not be enough but he wouldn't budge. They were two a penny he told her. Removing her wedding ring from her finger, Kate placed it on the counter. Picking it up, the pawnbroker looked at it closely through his eyeglass.

"It's gold," she said in an attempt to hurry him.

Five shilling was offered but she knew it was worth much more. Ten shilling, she asked.

He was not in the business of bartering but told her his final amount would be seven shilling and sixpence which she had no choice but to accept.

As soon as the paperwork was completed and the money counted out, Kate scooped it up into her purse. Hurrying down the road to the police station, she half ran, half walked in an effort to get there more quickly. She didn't care that people were staring at her.

A man, obviously drunk, was at the counter, slurring his words at the desk officer. She tried to interrupt but was asked to wait so placed the vase on the counter and her hand to her head, swaying as if to faint. Someone got her a chair and a glass of water but she jumped up as the drunk swung his arms wide, knocking the vase from the counter. Catching it in one hand, Kate fell to the floor, managing to save it from breaking. As she sat in a heap, she really did feel sick.

A constable helped her up, asking if he could be of

assistance so she explained about Clara. She was surprised to hear that they had been released earlier in the morning when the fine had been paid. He was unable to tell her who had paid the fine but all the ladies had been released.

Running home, Kate didn't care if people were looking at her now, she had to see if Clara had returned, but she wasn't waiting by the door. She felt deflated in the oppressive room, walls closing in as she was close to tears. Placing the vase back on the mantelpiece, she looked at Edward's picture. Remaining in her coat, she sat by the window waiting, just waiting, her mind going round and round. Whatever happened, she knew she would have to make things right with Clara or be left with nothing.

She was surprised when there was a light tap on the door. Clara stood in front of her, a little dishevelled but at least she was home. Kate's heart was pounding like waves surging against a cliff, so much so she couldn't speak. Opening the door wide, letting Clara in, they stood looking at each other. The silence said everything and nothing at the same time. She wanted to throw her arms around her and tell her she knew where she had been but did neither as she waited for Clara to speak.

The silence was deafening and uncomfortable so Kate spoke. "I'm sorry, Clara. I'm so sorry I slapped you. Can you forgive me?" Kate held her hands out to this complicated girl.

"Where's your wedding ring?" was the first thing Clara said, looking at the thin white band of skin on Kate's finger.

"I pawned it to pay your court fine. I saw you at the Town Hall," was all Kate said.

Both felt they had so much to say but nothing could heal the hurt they both felt and they were silent again.

Finally Clara asked, "Can I say my piece first?"

Kate nodded. It was the least she deserved.

"Why did you never explain to me I wasn't yours? I'd heard rumours over the years about Ted not being my father." As an afterthought she continued, "and his mother never liked me so I assumed it was because you had a relationship with someone else. You have lied to me all my life. Do you know how that feels?" Clara didn't wait for a response. "I'm not who I thought I was and neither are you. I can't even remember my real mother. She's never bothered about me, has she?"

The accusations and questions came at Kate like a gust of wind, abating temporarily before billowing again. She needed to salve her own conscience, never mind Clara's, but all she could say was, "I'm sorry, but not sorry that I think of you as my daughter."

Clara changed the subject. She couldn't ask any more about her mother.

"Well, as you are aware, I spent last night in a prison cell." Clara half smiled. "But Lady Evie paid our fines this morning and they let us go."

"Hang on, start at the beginning. That was last night. Where were you the night before?" Kate looked astonished. "And who on earth is this Lady Evie?"

Clara began her monologue, explaining to Kate she had walked up to Linthorpe Village to look at the old house before going to the cemetery to talk to Ted.

She'd stood there for a long time, until the cold reached her bones so she walked through Albert Park, asking Kate if she remembered the little café, but didn't wait for a response.

Although she had no money, she wanted to get warm, and saw a number of women sitting around the tables so went in to see what was happening.

It seems, she continued, that Lady Evie, Lady Evelyn Bellamy had just returned from London where her family had tried to forge an engagement with some idiot. That was the word she used, idiot. Well, she was having none of it because all her money would become his and that wasn't fair.

Kate struggled to see where this was leading but let Clara continue.

"While in London, Lady Evie had met women who were fighting for their rights but weren't getting very far. Anyway she thought it would be a good idea to have a march in Middlesbrough to support the sisters in London. Well, as I say, I went in and listened to her. She was very good at putting her point across. I just got caught up in the moment. You'll like this, she asked my name and asked if I was related to Sir Francis Williams, the ship builder. Well, I didn't know what to say so told her he was a very distant cousin. But you know my name isn't Williams. It shouldn't even be Stainbank but I don't know what it is."

Kate shook her head at what she had done, what she had allowed to happen. It had never really occurred to her what effect this would have on Clara, only her own feelings. This was something she just had to put right.

"Anyway," Clara continued, "we were all given a cup of tea and a teacake with lashings of butter and spent the night painting banners, trying to get some sleep though it wasn't very comfortable. I just went with the women as we marched to the Town Hall. Lady Evie stood on a box and started talking to whoever would listen about the plight of women. As you can imagine, there was a lot of heckling but she stood up for herself. Even when the men got bawdy, she gave as good as she got. Then the police turned up and I managed to catch one of them with my banner and knock his helmet off which didn't go down well. In the end, four of us including Lady Evie were arrested and left in the cells overnight. She paid our fines and we were let out this morning."

The room fell silent before both of them let out a belly laugh which continued until they were both crying. Kate wasn't sure who made the first move but suddenly they were hugging each other.

"You smell awful," she said to Clara which had them both

laughing again. "What happens now?" was all Kate could say before becoming tearful.

"Well, Lady Evie wants us to meet again later to sign a letter which she is going to take to the Prime Minister. Can you imagine that? She is thinking of taking some of us to London to present it to him."

"No, I mean what happens to us?" Kate asked, clutching at the girl's hands.

"Well, I did think I would try to find my father. He might have money and he owes me but I don't know how to go about it. But then I thought, I've got this far in my life without him, what good would it do. I don't think whoever it is would be interested in his flyblow turning up, especially as you thought he was a gentleman. I could write to Alice to ask her, I suppose."

"I don't know how forthcoming she would be and you will always be my daughter, Clara, and I couldn't love you more so can we draw a line under it and get on with the rest of our lives?"

"That's easy for you to say. I don't feel I belong anywhere and I do want to know more about the circumstances, you owe me that," Clara told her.

"Yes, yes, of course I will tell you all I know but first we need to find some money as I have no food in the house, no coal and none for rent and I need to get my wedding ring back from the pawnbrokers."

"I suppose I'm to blame for that as well. I could go up to the house and demand my few days' wages. I wasn't going to but we need it. Then see if I can get something else but I want to see Lady Evie later to see what she's about." Clara put on her coat again and went out of the door.

Kate didn't feel matters were sorted but at least they were talking, though Clara seemed to have hardened somehow. The room was quiet now she was on her own again. Whatever it took, she would talk to Clara. She would leave nothing out, if that's what it took to be friends again. They would find work of some kind, she was sure, and at least she didn't have children with croup or worse. Maybe her life wasn't so bad.

It was the early evening before Clara returned with a woman she introduced as Lady Evelyn Bellamy who Kate took an instant dislike to. The room was small, dark and dingy, Kate knew that, but she didn't want someone else to wrinkle their nose at it.

"We need help," Clara said. "The police are looking for us and we need to get away."

"What have you done?" Kate sat on the bed, offering the chairs to Clara and her guest.

"We have thrown eggs, flour and paint at the offices of the council officials to get their attention," Lady Evie said. "We need to get to London to my godfather's but can't go to the railway station. They will be looking for us there."

"You are only fifteen, Clara, just a child and very young to be going as far away as London." Kate looked at her.

"I think it's for the best. There is nothing here for me. Do you think Mr Thompson upstairs would be able to get us on a boat?" Clara continued.

"Nothing for you here? What do you mean? What about me? I'm your family," Kate cried.

"You can't stop me. You're not my mam!" Clara saw the hurt in Kate's eyes and she wanted her to hurt as much as she did.

The words cut Kate to the core and she knew she was beaten. "If you insist on this, I'll go and speak to Mr Thompson." Kate wanted to say how hurt she was but could see Clara was determined to strike out at her and at least she wouldn't be going away alone.

A few minutes later, Kate came back, saying there was a boat leaving later that evening taking coal from Durham. It didn't have any berths but no one would think to look for them there.

The three of them sat, not knowing what to say next.

"I'm sorry I can't offer you anything to drink," Kate said apologetically. Time went far too quickly. There was so much she wanted to say, should say but didn't want to make matters worse. Nor did she want to talk in front of this woman, Lady Evelyn, who she really didn't like.

It was a relief for all concerned when Mr Thompson knocked for them. He looked at Lady Evie's coat. "I wouldn't wear that, miss. It will be filthy with all the coal dust. Haven't you something darker to wear?"

Clara picked up Kate's coat. "Here, swap for this one. That's alright, isn't it?"

Kate watched as the young woman put on the tatty black coat, dropping the turquoise blue coat with fur trim round the collar and cuffs onto the bed like a rag. "I couldn't accept that. It's far too expensive." She was about to say more but Mr Thompson hurried them out.

"Can I come to the docks with you?" Kate asked.

"Better not," Clara replied.

"Will you at least write to me and tell me how you are?" Kate asked but received no response. She grabbed at Clara, trying to hug her, to stop her from leaving but was brushed away. She wanted to hang on to her legs, beg her not to go but couldn't.

CHAPTER 25

Then they were gone into the night. Kate closed the door and went to the bed in the corner of the room. How long she remained there she wasn't sure. She didn't move, afraid she would collapse into a thousand pieces. The silence screamed at her, only broken by the occasional sob as the tears rolled slowly from her long lashes, down her cheeks before dripping off the edge of her chin. There was no feeling in her legs while her fingers tingled with pins and needles so she knew she was still alive.

Her body was inert but her mind screamed at what had happened. She had accepted Clara's decision too easily. Should she have fought like a fishwife to keep her child with her? But that was it, she wasn't her child, was she? The crying started again. She was like a wounded animal. The pain in her chest threatened to overwhelm her such was her distress. All she wanted to do was retreat into a dark corner, out of sight, to lick her wounds in peace. Peace… would she ever know peace again? She thought she had reached her lowest ebb when her beloved Ted had died, or when Edward was lost to her but this felt like the end. Life was no longer worth living. If she had the energy, she would take herself to the River Tees and throw herself in, let the pain wash over her.

KATE LAY LISTENING for Mr Thompson's return the following morning. Hearing a key in the front door lock, she opened her own door. She didn't care that she looked a mess, skin pale, eyes red with crying.

"Did they get away alright, Mr Thompson?" Kate's voice was hoarse.

"Yes, it won't be a comfortable journey but it's only for a few days," he replied.

"Thank you so much for your help." Kate's knees almost buckled as she leant against the stanchion.

"Get yourself in, lass." Mr Thompson put his arm out to stop her falling. "Oh, look, I nearly forgot. Your girl gave me this to pass to you."

Kate looked at his outstretched hand with two shilling coins.

"Keep one for your trouble," she said, though she could ill afford.

"No, no, it's yours." He placed them both in her hand. "Now, if you'll excuse me, I must get some sleep."

Closing the door quietly, Kate went to where Edward's picture sat propped up against the Linthorpe vase, placing the two coins next to it before returning to the warmth of her bed where she finally slept.

Awaking more refreshed, Kate's mind immediately went to thoughts of Clara. She hadn't forgotten her. She had sent her money so all was not lost. She was hopeful that she would get in touch soon.

She felt foolish putting on the coat which had belonged to Lady Evelyn. It wasn't something people round here would wear. Putting the money off the mantlepiece in her purse with the seven and sixpence from her wedding ring, Kate went back to the pawnshop to get it back.

She had to pay an extra sixpence to the pawnbroker to get the ring back which she placed straight onto her finger where it belonged. That only left her with one and sixpence to buy food, not enough for rent. However, as she got back to the room, two police officers were standing outside.

"Mrs Williams?" the policeman asked.

"Yes, I'm Mrs Williams. How can I help you, constable?"

"We'd like you to accompany us to the station to answer some questions," he told her.

"What about? I've done nothing wrong." Kate was disturbed at what they wanted.

"We need to talk to you about harbouring criminals. I suggest you bring anything of value with you." The young man became more insistent. "You may be there awhile if you need to go to court."

"What criminals? I haven't done anything. I don't know what you are talking about." Kate began to panic. Unlocking the door, she showed the two men into the room. "You see, there is no one here, never has been, I live alone. Who do you think I'm hiding? It's hardly a place for muggers, maimers or murderers, is it?"

"We'd rather discuss this at the station, Mrs Williams."

Picking up the vase, photo and letters, she placed them in her basket. As an afterthought, Kate put her drawing pad and pencils in as well. Looking round, she thought there was nothing much for a life really.

At the station she was asked how she came to have such a coat but she couldn't say. Where was Lady Evelyn and her friends? Again Kate did not answer. She was taken to a cell where she sat waiting, for what she didn't know. For several days she was spoken to by the police sergeant but she could give no answers. While sitting in the cell, she wrote on her painting paper a letter for anyone. She didn't know who would care but she needed to do something.

Sitting in the cell, all Kate could think about was how she now had nothing, not even a home to return to as she couldn't pay the rent. At least she was given warm food, warmer than she had eaten in weeks. It was bland but she ate it all. The tin mug held a strong cup of tea which she relished.

She sat on the bed with her legs tucked under her, the coat keeping the chill off, which she was eternally grateful for at this moment. The sound of footsteps woke her. Her body ached from sitting but she forced herself to stand as the door opened.

"Time to go," the constable said as he stood aside to let her through the door.

She collected her basket from the front desk. A gentleman stood waiting, explaining he was her solicitor.

KATE THANKED the solicitor who had gained her release without criminal charges being brought against her.

"I have no money to pay you," she told him, embarrassed at her predicament.

"It's been taken care of Mrs Williams." He looked at her.

"By Lady Evelyn's parents?" she asked.

"No, I shouldn't say this but they have disowned her. It's her godfather who has provided the means to help her and you. Now, Mrs Williams, do you have anywhere to go?" He seemed concerned.

"It's a choice between the whorehouse and workhouse and the latter seems preferable at the moment." Kate felt her eyes well up at the thought of where her life had taken her.

"No family?" the solicitor asked.

"I need to find my daughter who has gone with Lady

Evelyn and a sister who is nursing in London but I have no means to get there."

"I can sort that if that is where you wish to go." For the first time, his whole face smiled, lighting up his eyes.

"I'm sorry, I'm not begging, sir. I'm more than grateful for your help." Kate picked up her basket.

"Wait a moment, Mrs Williams. Constable, let me have a pen and paper." The solicitor quickly wrote a note and took the envelope where he scribbled a name and address. "Come with me and I'll explain on the way." He took Kate's arm, nodding to the constable. They finally left the police station by the stairs and through the front door of the Town Hall.

The solicitor hailed a cab to take them the short distance to the railway station. She thanked him again. Kate couldn't believe her luck, someone was looking down on her, it didn't matter who it was, Ted, Edward, her parents, it didn't matter. Taking the letter of introduction and the purse full of coins, Kate walked onto the station platform with her back straight and her head held high, though she was shaking inside.

She remembered waving her parents off, John and Edward but there was no one to say goodbye to her. She longed to go to Ted's grave to talk to him because she was sure she would never be back in Middlesbrough again. She had been happy here until recently but now it was a new start, though what Rachel would say when she turned up goodness only knew.

Kate watched out of the window as the town disappeared into the smoke, the chimneys of the steelworks poking above before disappearing. As the train built up speed, she closed her eyes.

THE TRAIN BECAME BUSIER as they moved closer to London. Kate found herself crushed by the window as the carriage filled. She had no idea how much further she had to go.

When the train finally arrived, she became nervous as there were people hurrying everywhere, embarking on journeys on the waiting trains or rushing through the station. Everyone seemed to have somewhere to go except her. She didn't know which way to go. Spotting a gentleman in a railway uniform, she made her way toward him.

"Can you tell me where I can get a cab to this address," she asked, showing him the envelope the solicitor had given her.

Pushing his glasses further up the bridge of his nose, he looked at the now crumpled envelope. "Bloomsbury, take the left exit." His hand pointed. "You'll get a cab there. Don't let them charge you more than two shilling, mind."

Kate didn't understand all he said, he talked funny, but she was sure he said two shilling. After thanking him, she set off, still reeling at the cost. Luckily, there were a number of cabs waiting, she showed the first one the address.

"How much?" she asked.

"That'll be four shilling for you, madam."

"I'll not pay anything over two," she responded, pleased that the railway man had advised her.

The cabbie nodded. The smells and people were so different to home, Middlesbrough, but it was no longer home for her. She would never go back. There was nothing there for her other than Ted's grave and she hoped he would understand.

PART V

CHAPTER 26

KATE AND RACHEL 1902 LONDON

As the cab turned into Russell Square, Kate was surprised to see a large garden in the middle with houses all round the outside, making a square, hence the name. They stopped outside a terraced house which looked narrow though there were steps up to the front door and also down to the cellar below. Paying the cabbie the two shilling, which seemed a ridiculous amount for the distance, Kate didn't give a tip but stood on the pavement, looking at the front door, letter in hand, not really knowing how to explain why she was here. She ran up the steps, knocking on the door before her nerve left her. She had no idea what she was doing here but as she had run out of options, she felt there was nothing to lose.

Moving from one foot to the other, jumping when the door was opened, she waited as a servant looked her up and down. Passing the now crumpled envelope to the girl, Kate wondered if she was able to read and write.

"Wait here," the girl said, opening the door wider to let her enter.

The houses looked narrow from the outside but this tiled hallway was larger than the filthy room she had left behind.

There was a door on the left, the same side as the stairs, the other had two doors. A chandelier hung from the high ceiling, bringing dappled light to the black and white tiles. The first door on the right opened as the girl returned.

"Would you follow me. The mistress will see you now." The girl half bobbed her knee, making Kate almost let out a nervous laugh.

"Take Mrs Williams' coat, Emma," the woman sitting in the chair next to the fire said as she stood to receive Kate.

She didn't want to remove her coat, to show this elegant lady her drab work skirt and grubby blouse but felt it would be rude to refuse. The heat from the roaring fire in the ornate grate was enough to make Kate feel faint. Passing her basket to the girl, she removed the coat which wasn't even hers, moving toward the lady.

"Emma, bring some tea. Mrs Williams, it's so nice to meet you." The woman's eyes belied the sentiment. Offering Kate a seat, the lady continued. "I believe it's you we have to thank for aiding our errant god-daughter."

Kate realised she was being spoken to, somewhat overwhelmed. "Is my daughter Clara here?"

"I'm sorry, Mrs Williams, I should have introduced myself properly. How remiss of me. I'm Leonora Grey, my husband is Evelyn's god-father. They were here, Evie and Clara, but no longer."

"Where is she then?" Kate asked, alarmed.

"Evie was told by her father he would no longer condone her behaviour and has sent her off to her step-brothers in New Zealand. Clara is with her. Mrs Williams, are you unwell?"

Kate let out something between a groan and a scream, falling back in the chair. "She's only fifteen, a child," she sobbed. Kate couldn't believe what she was hearing. Clara, her daughter was on her way to the ends of the earth. She would never see her again. She would never make amends.

"There seems to be some misunderstanding here, Mrs Williams. Clara told us her mother was dead and you were an aunt who took her in."

The lady was looking at her. She had to speak. "It's complicated but I brought Clara up from a baby. She's a daughter to me." Kate began crying, putting her hands to her face but the tears continued.

"I think you've had a shock, Mrs Williams, perhaps you would like to go and rest for a while. My husband will be back later. He could explain better." Leonora Grey pulled a cord at the side of the fireplace.

Kate couldn't speak, only nod her head as she realised she was being dismissed. Her life seemed to be continually unravelling before her eyes. She didn't know how much more she could take.

The bedroom wasn't large. Kate gave a hollow laugh. It was palatial to her, dark wood furniture, highly polished. The window looked out to the back of the building though she couldn't see much as the night had drawn in. Why had Clara said her mother was dead? To her, Kate supposed, she was. She wouldn't remember her and Alice had never made any effort to contact her even on her birthday or Christmas.

That was her last thought as her eyes closed. The next thing she heard was a tapping which woke her, unaware for a moment where she was. The tapping became louder.

"Come in," she called, wondering how long she had slept. She had no idea.

The girl, Emma, came in. "Dinner will be in half an hour, madam. I've brought some water to wash."

"Thank you," was all Kate could say.

A short time later Kate stood in the hallway, not sure which door to open and whether it was polite to do so. Fortunately, the sitting room door opened where a portly gentleman greeted her warmly.

"Mrs Williams, how nice to meet you. I'm Thomas Grey.

You've already met my wife. Come, let's eat." He held out his arm for her. Walking into the dining room on the arm of Lord Grey, Kate wanted to laugh at the absurdity of it all. The dark wood table was set for six people each side, one chair at the top and one at the bottom. There was so much crockery, cutlery and glassware that she could almost hear the table groan, never mind the two elaborate candelabra positioned at either end, giving the room an eerie glow. Her hosts had dressed for dinner. The whole event seemed comical to her but if she started to laugh it would become hysterical. Her mind was on the edge as it was so she would have to contain herself. Fortunately, she didn't need to speak as yet another servant offered her wine. She rejected by a shake of her head.

Kate was offered a soup starter of which she accepted a small amount, watching the others to pick up the correct spoon. As quickly as it was finished, bowls were removed.

"I hope the room is comfortable for you, Mrs Williams," Lady Grey said.

"Oh yes, very much so, thank you for your hospitality," Kate replied, thinking of the cell and her previous room which were nothing more than middens.

Lord Grey waved for the servant to serve the next course. "The note said you are travelling to your sister. May I ask where that is?"

"She's at Rathbone Hall. It's a hospital for injured soldiers. It's at Millbank, on the Thames, but I don't know how far away that is." Kate realised she was rambling.

The servant offered her some mutton and vegetables but she couldn't eat. Her stomach was still complaining. The soup had been rich and creamy. It was the most she had eaten in days, no weeks, even months and she knew she couldn't take any more without making a fool of herself.

"Come now, Mrs Williams, you don't have to worry about that now. Are you not hungry, or does our offering not suit your palate?" Lord Grey asked. "I could ask cook to make you some eggs."

"No, no, sir, madam, I'm sure your food is delicious but I'm not very hungry," Kate replied.

"Perhaps you would rather retire to your room," Lady Grey said. "I could send Emma up with some tea and biscuits if you would prefer. It must have been an exhausting time for you and you will need to rest before your onward journey tomorrow."

"Oh, that would be lovely, thank you, if it's not too much trouble." Kate was relieved and stumbled as she rose.

Lord Grey caught her arm.

"Yes, I think it's all been overwhelming for you. We can talk at breakfast tomorrow." Lord Grey smiled. "I'm sure a good night's sleep would be beneficial."

Before the servant closed the dining room door, leaving Kate standing in the hallway, she heard Lady Grey say, "I don't know what Henry was thinking sending that woman to us. Her daughter was feral, but her!"

She didn't hear any more and wanted to go in and demand what right they had talking about her like that but didn't want to be thrown out on the street at this time of night. She hadn't always been down. At the time she was married to Ted, they had thought themselves well off. Nothing like those two in the dining room but they were comfortable. She was determined not to get upset as she made her way up the stairs, but felt overwhelmed and weary to her bones.

The poor girl, Emma, came up with a tray. She looked at Kate's red eyes. "Oh miss, madam, don't get upset. The Mrs's bark is worse than her bite."

"It's not that. I'm sure both are kindly enough but I don't belong here. I've lost everything and I don't know what to do about it," Kate sobbed.

"Well as cook says, tomorrow is another day and a nice

cup of tea solves all sorts of problems." Emma placed the tray the small table by the window.

Once Kate was alone again, she sighed deeply. She needed to get an address for Clara and contact her as soon as possible, to let her know she loved her. Sipping her tea, she thought Emma was right, it does calm the nerves and make you feel better, and the biscuits were a bonus.

A GOOD NIGHT'S sleep helped Kate to feel more herself the following morning. She even smiled when she thought she had gone full circle from the lovely house she shared with Ted and her family to a prison cell in Middlesbrough and to this huge house in London if only for one night.

The dining room had an array of silver dishes on a sideboard. Lord Grey was already at the table though his wife was nowhere to be seen. "Ah, Mrs Williams, good morning. I hope you slept well? Please help yourself and join me."

"Good morning, sir, thank you once again for your hospitality," Kate responded, placing some scrambled eggs on a plate. She couldn't face the liver. Once she was seated and a pot of tea put in front of her, Lord Grey dismissed the servant.

"Could you tell me exactly what happened to Evelyn and your daughter, Mrs Williams, and how you ended up in that dreadful prison. The note was a little sketchy," Lord Grey asked.

Kate told him what she knew and the fact that both girls had been involved in breaking windows at the Town Hall. The police were looking for them for criminal damage. She had managed to get them on a boat from the docks to London but had been arrested for harbouring criminals. The police had no evidence other than the coat Lady Evelyn had given her.

Lord Grey listened intently. "My god-daughter is very headstrong, as I'm sure you realise. Her parents despair of her ever finding a husband who could control her. That's why they sent her off to New Zealand. Her step-brother is in the Government there. I'm sure your daughter will be well looked after."

"Clara is angry with me and I need to put that right. Do you have an address where I can write to her? She is still only a child as I explained to your wife yesterday," Kate told him.

Lord Grey stood and walked over to a bell pull, where a servant arrived almost immediately. "Could you get me pen and paper and arrange a cab for Mrs Williams to go to Rathbone Hall."

When the servant came back, Lord Grey wrote out a note and sealed it in an envelope on which he wrote an address.

"Now I'm sorry, Mrs Williams, but I must be on my way." He shook Kate's hand, giving her the envelope. "Emma will assist you with your belongings. I hope everything works out to your satisfaction."

With that, Kate was yet again dismissed, but waited until Lord Grey left the room before going back up the stairs to the bedroom for her meagre basket of belongings. She didn't know what to do about the coat but couldn't travel without one. Putting it on over her dirty, dowdy skirt, she felt much better. It was warm and the colour highlighted the colour of her eyes. It was, it seemed to her, like a cloak of respectability.

CHAPTER 27

Kate caught sight of Rathbone Hall towering out of the early morning mist, a magnificent building with a long driveway. The cab didn't continue in that direction but turned off the road halfway along, taking her past a lake and huge gardens. It came to a stop outside a much smaller building built of the same stone, more like a farmhouse with outbuildings nearby. In front of the house was a garden with several tables, chairs and benches dotted about. Trees grew proud, offering shade and leading back toward the lake. Men in uniform were sitting about even though there was a chill in the air. Kate stepped down, breathing deeply as she watched the cab turn round. Now she was alone. If Rachel wasn't here then she was stuck. Shaking herself, she walked up the steps and through the open door into the hospital.

"Can I help you?" a woman's voice came from the room on the left.

"I'm looking for Rachel Stainbank. Is it possible to have a word with her? I'm her sister," Kate told her.

"I'll go and see if I can find her," the woman replied.

It wasn't what Kate thought of as a hospital, not like the one in North Ormesby where Ted had been. This was a house, a large house granted, but it didn't have that smell of antiseptic or cabbage.

She continued to stand, looking out of the window. Men in bathchairs or on crutches, limbs missing, were talking, smoking, laughing. She couldn't comprehend how they could laugh when they were crippled, in that terrible state. She was brought out of her thoughts.

"Kate, Kate, what on earth are you doing here?" Rachel moved toward her when she looked as though she might fall.

Kate rushed into her arms, crying, "I didn't know where else to go. I've lost everything, everything, even Clara."

"Sit down before you fall down. You're all skin and bone. Now, would you like to tell me exactly what brings you here?" Rachel smiled.

A great sob came from Kate as she tried to explain. "Clara knows about Alice. She's gone to New Zealand."

"Who? Clara or Alice?" Rachel looked confused.

"Clara. I've lost her. She's gone with Lady Evelyn Bellamy," Kate cried, snot running down her nose.

"You've lost me now. Who's that? What's she got to do with Clara? Oh, never mind, you'll have to start at the beginning but let me get you a cup of tea, and stop crying, you'll make your face all puffy," Rachel told her. "Wait here."

"No, no, Rachel, don't leave me here. I had no one else to go to. Don't you see, all I've got is what's in the basket." Kate grabbed her arm.

"Look, Kate, I'm working. Let me get you a drink. Stay put. I'll be back in a few minutes." Rachel went toward the door.

"Do you always talk so brusquely? It's more like an order than conversation," Kate said, attempting to lift the mood.

"I've got to keep the men in check. I'm not their love or

darling and I have to treat them like their mother or nanny," Rachel replied.

After what seemed like hours, Rachel returned with a cup of tea. "I've put plenty of sugar in, you look like you need it. The Captain, Captain Gibson Park, who owns the house has said you can stay, for a short while anyway. So come on, spit it out." Rachel looked directly at Kate. "And stop crying 'cause I can't understand a word you're saying."

Kate told her story for what felt like the hundredth time, including how she was now homeless, penniless, alone and why.

Rachel didn't say a word until Kate finished. "I knew this would come back to bite you. Didn't I tell you years ago, you needed to tell Clara about Alice." Rachel looked at her sister. "Oh, stop crying, Kate, you are stronger than this. Have you been in touch with Alice to let her know?"

"No, I haven't had time. I came to London straight from prison," Kate stated.

Rachel didn't speak for a moment before bursting out laughing loudly. "Do you know how absurd that sounds? Good thing mam and dad aren't around."

"If they were, I would have gone to them, wouldn't I? What am I going to do with myself?" Kate asked.

"Look, you're better off than half the lads here, so think on. I've arranged a bed to be put in my room for you. I'll show you where that is but I must get back to work. Perhaps you could go for a walk or something to clear your mind. Be warned, the men will rib you ceaselessly if they see a chink in your armour," Rachel told her.

KATE SAT on the edge of the bed, thankful Rachel had taken control. She felt so depressed, on edge, nervy… she didn't know what to call it. Her mother would have said she was at the end of her tether and she was right. When she looked at those poor men, Kate felt guilty. How long she remained sitting in the small room thinking, she didn't know, but shadows had moved, making it look gloomy as well as austere. She wondered if Rachel had always lived like this. She jumped when the door burst open and there she was.

"Now all of these are second-hand but clean and they will do you for now," she said as she placed clothes and towels next to Kate. "I'm not being funny but when was the last time you had a bath?"

"I don't ever remember you being so forthright." Kate tried to smile but her eyes filled with tears. "Or…" She didn't finish.

"Or rude, is that what you were going to say?" Rachel finished for her. "I didn't get this far by being nice. No one ever took notice of me when we were children," she continued. "It was always clever Kate or bonny baby Alice but no one ever said a word about me. Even the monster Frank got more of a mention. I always knew I wanted to get away. I never had the urge to marry, though I have had a number of proposals over the years, nor have children. Spinster of the parish, that's me." How many times had she said that, she lost count.

A tear rolled down Kate's cheek. She had never known Rachel had felt like this. She now felt a surge of grief for her sister who had never had the love of a good man like Ted Williams.

"Stop with the tears, they don't work here. Come with me for something to eat and I'll help you carry up some buckets of hot water from the kitchen so you can get a bath." Rachel opened the door.

"Help yourself," Rachel told her as they picked up a plate, "but whatever you put on a plate you eat."

It was when they were talking over the meal that Rachel completely took Kate by surprise. "You could go to New Zealand, have you thought of that? You're still a young woman, you could start again."

Kate was shocked and surprised. It had never occurred to her, but that was where her family were. Where Clara had gone. "I couldn't, Rachel, I couldn't go all that way on my own."

"Well, I don't know why not. It could be an option. You always got on with John," Rachel said in her matter of fact way.

"I wouldn't want to be a burden on them, and anyway I don't have the money for a passage." Kate was overwhelmed by the thought of going all that way by ship. She thought she had done well to get to London but that had been arranged for her.

"I could lend you the money if that's what you want to do. You don't have to make a decision now, just think about it. You'll have to earn your keep while you're here but there are more important things to get on with." Rachel grinned.

"What's that?" Kate asked, putting her plate on the trolley.

"You having a bath." Rachel laughed loudly. "Oh, come on, Kate, lighten up. The lads'll eat you for breakfast if you don't."

They carried two buckets of water each along the corridor and up the stairs to the small bedroom, trying not to spill any. Rachel went for the tin bath which was hanging on a nail behind the closet door at the room at the end of the landing. She wedged it in the corner by the window, which was the only place big enough, and emptied two buckets of hot water into it.

"Right, strip down to your underwear and I'll wash your hair before I go back downstairs," Rachel told her, grabbing the bar of carbolic soap. "I'll leave you to wash in peace. Get one of the buckets and take the water to the end room. Use one to put in your clothes to soak. When I get back, I'll need to sleep. I'm up at five in the morning."

"Yes, miss." Kate saluted while removing her dirty blouse and skirt. She could smell sweat, coal, urine on herself and felt ashamed. Rachel was rough washing her long hair and she wanted to shriek at the pain but it was the closest anyone had been to her in a long time and she was determined not to cry anymore.

With her hair wrapped in one of the worn towels, Kate removed the rest of her clothes, sitting in the warm water though it was no longer clean. She scrubbed with the piece of rag until her skin was pink and glowing. Then she lay there, savouring the warm steam until the water began to cool.

The nightdress felt lovely on Kate's still damp skin as she carried buckets of dirty water to the closet, rinsing them out before filling one with cold water to put in her underclothes, stockings, blouse. Her skirt was too thick. Rubbing her hair dry, she felt much better than she had in months. If only she could sort things out with Clara. She wasn't going to think about that now, only happy thoughts. She had been well fed, she was clean and she had a bed… what more could she ask for at this moment.

She didn't hear Rachel come into the room, nor go out again the following morning. It was sunlight falling across her face which woke her.

SUDDENLY KATE WAS BUSY. She was in the kitchen laundry, putting sheets into the poss tubs, throwing bloodied bandages into another to boil. As quickly as she managed to fold and roll clean ones onto a trolley, there were more waiting to be washed. It was hard work. With her arms up to her elbows in soap suds, she dunked and swirled the sheets and bandages with the bleached white wooden posser, rolling them through the mangle. They were rinsed in clean water before being hung out in a yard, when she could, on rows and rows of clothes lines.

Her shoulders and back were in competition to see which hurt most and she was glad of her bed each evening. Although the days were hard physically, Kate was eating better, and the gaunt, haunted look left her face.

CHAPTER 28

Kate eventually found time to sit in the garden, late one afternoon, where she penned letters to both Clara and John. The latter was easier to write, explaining she was now living at the hospital with Rachel and why. She asked if it would be possible for John and Ellen to be there with Clara when she read her letter in case she needed support or confirmation of what she had written.

The letter to Clara was much more difficult, taking many attempts before she got the tone of it to her satisfaction. Kate didn't want it to be gloomy or too upsetting. She finished it by hoping Clara would forgive her and find happiness. If she needed family around her, she was sure John and Ellen would be only too happy to take her in. Maybe it would be nice to spend time with her cousins Elodie and Christa. After all, there were only a few years between them.

More importantly if at anytime she was unhappy, Kate would welcome her home. Kate didn't say she didn't know where that would be but that she would welcome her with open arms.

She found a box to put the letters in along with the vase. John still had the other one and she hoped Clara would think of her when she saw it. Someone would post it for her when they went into the town.

Leaning back in the chair, she closed her eyes, allowing the sun to fall on her face. The warmth was beginning to fade but she wanted to enjoy it for a few moments more. The place seemed tranquil somehow, letting minds and bodies recover from the horrors before. Kate wasn't putting her own trouble in the same place as the poor men here, but she could see why it was so important for them to heal. It wasn't really a hospital, it was more a place of sanctuary, camaraderie and hope, yes, that was it, a place of hope.

Kate jumped when a burst of laughter rang out, followed by the bell for their evening meal. Some of the men watched her with interest, and she was relieved when they gave her space. She didn't feel ready to be the object of fun just yet.

She knew it could take six months to get a reply to her letters so life would have to go on. The only way to make it better was to become more involved with life here, after all she had nowhere else to go.

The place wasn't busy as the men more or less looked after themselves, other than the nursing side which Rachel did with another nurse, Amy Elicotte. There was a cook and two kitchen helpers where Kate spent much of her time. Those who could do, helped those who couldn't, so Kate realised it wasn't a hospital but more of a home for injured soldiers.

The ground floor had a kitchen and dining room where they all ate together. Kate saw that what would have been called a parlour had been turned into a bedroom with two rows of beds for the men. On the other side of the hallway was a room where they could sit more comfortably as well as the small office where she found herself the day she arrived. Up the wide staircase the floor went both left and right. To the right Captain Gibson Park had a bedroom, with an informal parlour. The other room was for his valets who seemed to do all his caring. Kate hadn't yet met him as Rachel had warned her to give him a wide berth. He didn't want company.

The rooms on the left were for the rest of the staff. Cook had a room of her own while the two kitchen assistants shared a larger room. Rachel and Amy had rooms to themselves. She had never ventured up the steep staircase to the attic so had no idea what was up there.

Days seemed to go quickly into weeks, then months as Kate realised she was content in this house of men. She couldn't say she was happy as something was missing, love and to be loved, but content was a good word. She slept much better, the food was plain but plentiful, most of it from the cottage garden at Rathbone Hall. Her grey pallor had left her, as had the dark circles under her eyes. She was still thin but her face didn't look gaunt anymore.

She had very little money left from the bag the solicitor had given her, and the only ones who were paid were the nurses, Rachel and Amy Elicotte as well as Mary Fergus, the cook. It didn't matter to Kate, after all she had nowhere to spend it, though she thought better clothes would be nice. She knew she was lucky. She could have ended up in the workhouse where she would be far worse off. She was warm, well fed and had become much closer to Rachel. They often talked of an evening while sitting in bed with a warm drink.

It was one of those evenings when Rachel broached the subject of New Zealand again.

"I'm not ready to think about it," Kate told her. "Maybe once I've received a letter from John or Clara, I'll be able to think. Why?"

"Things have settled down here. There isn't much nursing to do. The men look after each other. I was thinking of going back to Durham to either teach or train to become a matron," Rachel told her.

"Oh no, I feel I was just getting to know the real Rachel," Kate responded. "What will happen to me?"

"I was thinking about it before you came. I haven't mentioned it to anyone else. I'll need to speak to the Captain for a reference anyway, when he's in a good mood," Rachel said.

"Perhaps I'll have to do the same. If I can't stay here, I'll need a letter of introduction at least," Kate replied, somewhat perplexed. "Let's enjoy Christmas together before you make a decision. How about that."

Rachel agreed and they both settled down.

For the first time in weeks, Kate couldn't sleep, worrying about where she could go if Rachel left. Did she want to stay here without her sister? What would she do if she was thrown out? She had no money and nowhere to go. It had to be sorted.

She lay on the verge of sleep when she heard a screaming and yelling. She turned over just as Rachel got up, putting on her dressing gown.

"What's going on, Rachel?" she asked.

"I'll tell you when I get back," Rachel replied, going quietly down the corridor.

Kate lay waiting. She was wide awake now, wondering if she should go and see if she could help.

Rachel returned about half an hour later. "It's alright, it happens now and then," she told Kate, getting back into her now cold bed. "The men have nightmares sometimes, about what went on in battle. They think they're still there where they've seen men speared and shot in front of them. Some are only boys." She stopped when she remembered her nephew, Edward.

"It must be awful to still feel like that after all this time." Kate was also thinking of her boy.

"Yes, well, the physical side heals, but the Captain has more problems than most as he blames himself for the men he lost. That's the reason he won't go downstairs. He can't face them," Rachel told her. "Now let's try and get some sleep."

THE FOLLOWING morning while they were sitting eating breakfast, one of the workers from the Hall rushed in, asking for help. There had been an accident, in the cottage garden, with a scythe and the man was bleeding heavily. They had sent for a doctor but he could be a while. Rachel grabbed a bag with bandages and antiseptic. Freddie Stewart and Archie Watkins, the Captain's two valets offered to go with Rachel in case the man needed to be brought back. However, the Captain was still asleep after last night's nightmare and they worried about no one being around if he awoke.

Kate offered to sit with him so the three of them rushed off. The Captain lay in his bed while Kate looked at the view. From the window, she could see Rathbone Hall, smoke spiralling up to the clouds from numerous chimneys. It looked as though someone had waved a huge hand through the smoke, sending it in all directions when the wind caught it, trees bowing, leaves dancing and swirling before falling to the ground. It seemed somehow poetic but she knew it would be cold out there today. The Captain's brother was Lord of the Manor but she had never met him when he called to visit. He was the only visitor who came regularly other than the vicar but she saw him every Sunday when she attended the local church.

As she was about to take a seat by the window, the Captain awoke. "Who are you? How long have you been here?" he asked rather gruffly.

"I'm Kate Williams, Nurse Stainbank's sister," Kate told

him. "Do you mean how long have I been in this room or here in this house?"

"Both, I suppose, where's Freddie and Archie?" the Captain asked, sitting up with his back against his pillows.

"Quite a lot of questions." Kate smiled, pouring him a glass of water and passing it to him. "The men are attending an accident at Rathbone Hall so I offered to sit with you. I hope that's alright? Would you like some breakfast? I could pop down and get you something?"

"Yes, thank you. Is that your way of getting out of answering any more questions?"

"No, of course not, though my life isn't that exciting," Kate replied. She didn't really want to go through how she had ended up here.

THE CAPTAIN WAS STILL SITTING up in his bed when she returned with a tray. Cook had made bacon, eggs and toast with a large pot of tea. Kate had hoped he would now be sitting in the bathchair and taken himself to the small table by the window.

"Oh look," she said as she put the tray down. "They are coming back with a cart. Perhaps they are bringing the patient here." Placing the tray on his knee, Kate stood looking at him while he looked at the tray. "Do you want me to pour?" she asked but he didn't answer as Freddie Stewart walked in, his hair ruffled from the wind.

"Thank you for your help, Mrs Williams. I can take over now." He grinned at Kate who couldn't help but smile back.

As she left the room, the Captain called her back. "I'd love to hear your story, Mrs Williams, perhaps tomorrow?"

"Perhaps we can trade each other's stories, Captain. I'd look forward to that." Kate laughed, going down the stairs to look for Rachel.

Kate walked to church each Sunday wearing the blue coat

which really belonged to Lady Evelyn Bellamy but she had nothing else. She felt overdressed compared to the other women. The men who chose to attend church wore their uniform and always looked smart. She always prayed for Ted, Edward and her parents but also Clara, wherever she was. It was as they walked back from the small village church that Kate always seemed to be in the company of Freddie Stewart. She enjoyed his easy manner. He was always very attentive, listening, her talking about nothing, anything in general.

"How come you came to be here?" Kate asked him.

"There were nine of us in the family, all starving, so as soon as I was old enough, I joined the army to ease the burden. Family died of typhoid and I had nowhere to go when I came back to England. I was lucky having the Captain as my officer. He offered me a chance here otherwise I would have probably ended up in the workhouse," Freddie told her.

"I'm sorry to hear about your family, that must have been terrible for you," Kate told him. "I've got a brother and his family in New Zealand and a sister in Stafford but don't hear from her. Rachel is the closest to me." She wasn't ready to tell him about Clara or Edward or even Ted, though she was sure he would be sympathetic.

Kate spent much of her time helping in the kitchen because she didn't seem to have a particular role. She would just try to keep busy and fit in with whatever needed doing. A few of the men had gone out to collect crab apples. Kate had peeled and cored the washed fruit, removing the seeds. She had put them to cook in a large pan with sugar, standing stirring while chatting with cook, Mary Fergus, who had her hands in a bowl making pastry for a pie. She told Kate she had gone to work at Rathbone Hall as a child, first in the laundry but was taught how to cook while there. She had been happy to move here with the Captain as he was always a favourite of hers.

Freddie came into the kitchen, asking if Kate would go and see the Captain but she had to refuse. She didn't want to spoil the apple jelly which was just coming to the boil. He took a seat at the end of the table when cook poured him a cup of strong stewed tea.

"How's the Captain today?" Mary Fergus asked.

"Just the same, Mary. He won't come downstairs and, believe me, I've tried. He's got a stubborn head so what can I do?" Freddie told her.

"Why won't he come downstairs?" Kate asked, puzzled.

"Thinks he's let the men down and no amount of talking makes any difference. It's all in his head but what can I do except pander to him." Freddie stood up. "I'll tell him you're waiting for the biscuits to cool," he said, looking at the row on the cooling tray.

That was how it started. Kate would be summoned to the Captain's room on an almost daily basis, where she had more contact with Freddie and Alfie. She had warmed to the three of them for different reasons. She knew they would be listening when she sat talking to the Captain and was happy about that. It meant she could tell those in the house without having to repeat herself over and over.

She would take up a tray of tea and biscuits or scones and they would sit in each other's company at the table by the window. Kate would pour tea and butter scones. The Captain would be washed and dressed, sitting in his bathchair with a rug over his legs.

"I was the second son. My brother Henry is Lord of Rathbone Hall. I was brought up there until I was nine when I was sent to boarding school. I hated it even though Henry was already there," the Captain told her. "Your turn."

Kate told him of the family's move to Middlesbrough where she worked with her father and brother at Linthorpe Pottery.

"I was expected to join the army or ministry because

Henry would inherit the title. I chose the army because I wasn't religious at that point. Your turn," he said again.

Although Kate enjoyed these meetings, they were sociable, genteel events but the Captain always wanted more of her than she was prepared to give. After each chat, Freddie Stewart always sought her out to make sure she was happy. He talked to her a little about his time in the army where he had been in South Africa. Kate told him she was a widow and was determined to ask him about where Edward was buried. She enjoyed his company. It felt like she was talking to her brother John. Someone who would look out for her.

It was as she was chatting to the Captain just a few weeks before Christmas that Kate broached the subject of why the men didn't do anything to earn a wage. They didn't have any money of their own.

"You don't know men very well, Mrs Williams. If I gave them money, they would be off to the local hostelry getting drunk and fighting amongst themselves or with the locals. It would give the place a bad name," the Captain told her.

"Yes, I see, I hadn't thought of that, but surely they need to do something to keep them occupied," Kate said.

"Any suggestions?"

"Well, you have a couple of small buildings which could be turned into a workshop. What about painting or making fences from willow. Farmers are always wanting fencing. You could ask the men?" Kate suggested.

"Has someone put you up to this to get me out of this room? The doctor, perhaps, or my brother, or even those two listening in next door." The Captain pointed a finger at the adjoining door.

"No, no, of course not, but it can't be healthy for you or the men to be sitting about all day." Kate wished she hadn't said anything.

"Mrs Williams, you know nothing of army life. The men think of their officers as supreme beings sent down from high to defend them. To take them into battle and keep them safe. But I didn't do that." He was shouting now. "Do you hear? I didn't do that! They followed me into battle where they died, killed, murdered, call it what you will. Those left will never be the same again. Now leave me. Go on, leave me!"

Kate rushed out of the room in tears. She knew nothing of his life, but she knew this is what must have happened to Edward. Her boy was dead, murdered, killed because someone hadn't done their job to keep him safe. She ran through the kitchen, opening the door to the laundry and outside where she sat on the step, sobbing. Someone sat next to her and she didn't flinch or freeze as he placed an arm around her shoulders which she found comforting and was grateful for.

"Don't let him upset you. He wants to lash out at anyone because he isn't happy," Freddie told her.

Kate nodded. "My son, Edward… he was killed in South Africa. He was just a boy," she sobbed. "He only joined up to help me out because there was no work." She lay her head on his shoulder as he held her close. How long they sat like this she wasn't sure but she didn't want to spoil the feeling of being safe.

Eventually both moved uncomfortably on the cold step and the spell was broken. Brushing down her skirt, Kate tried to smile.

"Best go and sort the old buggar out," Freddie laughed. "He'll be in a foul mood the rest of the day and take it out on all of us in one way or another. Well, I suppose that's his prerogative as it's his house. I'll be walking on eggshells in case he throws me out."

"Oh, don't say that. It's my fault. I shouldn't talk so freely to him but I thought that was what he wanted." Kate thought it might be her thrown out.

"Wish me luck. I'll see you later." Freddie left her.

CHAPTER 29

Kate wasn't summoned up to see the Captain again which was just as well. The doctor had been to give him something for his head pain whilst she was helping to prepare for Christmas. The day was cold and crisp but she felt she needed to get out into the fresh air. Picking up her coat, she told Mary, "I'll go and see if I can find some holly and ivy for table decorations, if you can manage?"

"Go on, take those two with you," Mary said, nodding toward the two girls. "They need to get out more, it's not good for them to be stuck in all day."

It wasn't long before the girls were stamping their feet, blowing on their hands with breath almost freezing. Kate sent them back with the ivy she'd found but was determined to pick holly to go with it. Wandering along the hedgerows, her mind miles away, thinking of her life, she didn't hear the passing carriage until it was almost on top of her. The only place she could go was the ditch where she fell unceremoniously as it carried on. She was struggling to get up, cuts and scratches on her hands and face, as a hand reached out, helping her to get back to a standing position.

"You could have been killed there," Freddie told her.

Brushing detritus from her coat, Kate replied, "What are you doing here? A knight in shining armour saving a damsel in distress?"

Freddie brushed leaves from her hair. "There's a letter arrived for you. I thought you'd want to know straight away. The girls told me where you were."

Kate hardly heard the last of the conversation as she picked up her skirt, ignoring the blood on her hand, and ran back toward the house. Freddie was left in her wake as he picked up the holly before following her into the kitchen. She didn't want to read the letter in front of the others so took herself up to her bedroom where she sat on the bed, hands shaking. She didn't know if this was because of the fall, running or the letter. It didn't matter. It was thick, Ellen's writing... they must have replied almost immediately.

Opening the envelope, Kate saw the letter she had written to Clara inside, with just two pages to Ellen's letter. She couldn't believe what she was reading. Clara wasn't there. She wasn't in New Zealand with Lady Evelyn Bellamy.

Rushing out of the door and down the stairs, she went to look for Rachel who she found just finishing re-doing the bandages on the man injured with the scythe.

Waving the two pieces of paper, Kate said, "She's not there. Clara didn't go to New Zealand."

"Where is she then?" Rachel took the letter from her.

"She got off the ship in Port Elizabeth. She's in South Africa," Kate said, her voice almost a scream.

Rachel scanned her eyes down the letter. "Says here she had a difference of opinion with this Lady Evelyn and took a post as companion to a Mrs Benson, wife of Captain Benson."

"Yes, yes, I read all that but she won't know where I am, nor I her. Oh God, what am I going to do?" Kate shouted.

"Don't have a go at me," Rachel snapped. "Look, she's found herself another job. It's her life."

"Clara's only a child. She shouldn't be making these decisions on her own. What if she writes to my old address and doesn't get a reply? She'll think I've abandoned her." Kate snatched the letter back from Rachel.

"Don't be so dramatic, Kate. Go and calm down. I'll talk to you later." Rachel left her sister open mouthed.

Kate wasn't sure whether her face and hands were smarting because of the scratches and scrapes or her tears but went to the bathroom to wash them anyway. She would have to try to find where Clara was. That child had been a worry from the day she was born, but she was her daughter and she loved her.

Taking a deep breath and smoothing her hair, she went back into the kitchen to help Mary. She told her briefly what was in the letter, but there was no point expanding on the whys and wherefores, it had nothing to do with her.

"The Captain might be able to help with an address," Mary told her. "He might even know this Captain Benson."

"Oh yes, of course, thanks Mary, I hadn't thought of that. I'll go and ask him later," Kate replied.

"It might be better to ask Archie or Freddie to broach it with the Captain, you know how he gets," Mary said. "Now get that bread out of the oven before it burns."

Kate was still angry at Rachel's attitude to the letter, making her determined not to discuss it any further with her unless she asked. There was no point as there was nothing she could do until after the festive season was over. Anyway, she would need to ask Rachel for money for a stamp so needed to be on good terms with her.

Christmas Day morning, Kate went to church with the

others and this time her prayers were all for Clara, to bring her home safely. Or at least to find out where she was.

As soon as she got back to the house, she was busy bringing food into the very festive dining room where the holly and ivy was festooned along the picture rail and decorated the table. Everyone seemed to have a lovely time and she thought they were really like an extended family all coming together for a special day. The men helped to carry crockery back to the kitchen before going for a smoke in the lounge while Kate helped the girls with the mountains of washing up.

New Year's Eve was even better as they had all been invited to a staff party at Rathbone Hall where they would eat, drink and dance into the New Year.

Kate saw the old Rachel, dancing, singing and joking with everyone. She was comfortable in anyone's company where Kate felt more reserved and out of place. Kate didn't want a drink but did have a number of dances with several men including Freddie Stewart. The loneliness of a life which had once enveloped her had abated. For the first time in years, she had laughed in a man's company. She felt she had known him years instead of months and was completely at ease with him.

It was a cold, clear early morning, stars blinking in the black sky as they walked back along the path. Each and every one tired and quiet as they hurried toward a warm bed for some welcome sleep.

As the two women were getting into bed, Rachel said, "You're not the only one who got a letter. I've got a place on a course in Durham. I'm going to see the Captain tomorrow to tell him I'm leaving. I'll speak up for you, Kate, but I have to go."

"Spoil the moment why don't you? Oh, I'm sorry but you seemed so happy tonight. Do you think you're making the right choice?" Kate asked sleepily.

"I need to be useful, fulfilled and I don't feel that here anymore. We'll talk more tomorrow. Now, let's try to get a few hours' sleep," Rachel said.

Kate was sure everyone heard the Captain shouting at Rachel, who came straight back to the bedroom.

"He's not happy about me leaving even though I tried to explain that there was only enough work for one nurse and Amy was happy to stay. He wants you out as well so we've got till the end of January to find something for you. I'm sorry!" Rachel grabbed Kate's hand.

"I'll find somewhere to go but I may have to borrow some money from you until I get settled," Kate replied but wasn't very confident at that moment.

It was as Kate was in the kitchen trying to peel vegetables, talking to Mary that Freddie blustered into the room.

"Can I have a word, Kate?" He nodded toward the back door. Sitting on the cold step as they had before, he said, "I found out earlier you'll be leaving so I've told the Captain I'll be going with you."

"You can't do that. I've nowhere to go." Kate looked at him. "Where will you go? Oh, Freddie what have you done?"

"Here's the thing, Kate. I was wanting to make my own way but this has made me realise I need to do it now. No, listen, let me have my say." Freddie took hold of her hand. "If you'll have me, we could make a life together for better or worse."

"Are you asking me to marry you?" Kate looked into his face as his eyes sparkled.

"Yes, and before you answer, let me explain. On New Year's Eve, I was talking to old George, the groundsman at Rathbone Hall. Well, he's retiring and they're looking for someone to take over." He paused for breath. "I rushed over this morning to see Lord Henry Gibson Park, he knows me, and I've got the job."

"Well done, Freddie. I'm pleased for you," Kate told him, still holding his hand.

"That's not all, there's a cottage goes with it. It hasn't been lived in for a while and needs a good clean but don't you see, we could live there and I'd get a wage. What do you say? We could put the banns up now and marry in three weeks before Rachel goes." His face lit up. "Will you, Kate? Will you marry me?"

His question had thrown her and now she had to be careful how she answered. It would certainly solve her homeless problem and she liked him well enough. Enough to marry him?

She looked at his expectant face.

"You've caught me by surprise. It sounds too good to be true. It's wonderful but we hardly know each other." She tried to say it softly.

"What do we need to know? We're not young people having to save for several years, are we? We've got nothing now so it can only get better." He started to laugh. "I'm not selling myself very well, am I? I really care about you, Kate, and I'm sure it will grow into love. How can it not? You're lovely."

"Thank you, Freddie, and that's how I feel about you, but are you sure? All I've got is what I'm wearing and most of that's second-hand." Kate moved closer to him where they kissed, arms around each other.

"Is that a yes then?" he asked.

"Yes, yes, it is." Kate grinned at him.

GRABBING THEIR COATS, they rushed off to see the vicar about putting up the banns before going to look at the cottage at the other side of Rathbone Hall. It was the middle of three very small cottages, and when Freddie forced the door open, they saw it was one up, one down with a garden at the front.

It didn't look as though it had been lived in for a long while but at least there was no smell of damp. The fire doubled up as the cooking facilities with a bread oven on one side and hooks and trivet on the other. Water was from an outside tap. The only furniture in the small room was a table and two kitchen chairs. There was little more than a ladder up to the roof space. Freddie climbed up and he shouted that there was a bed though the mattress had seen better days and a couple of clippie mats on the bare floor.

Kate stood looking around, asking herself could she live here with this man? She didn't want to say yes because it was her only option, so she said yes because she thought she could. Brushing a cobweb from his hair, she moved toward him. They kissed with more urgency, holding each other tightly. Kate liked the closeness of this man. He would never be Ted, that would be impossible, but as she thought when she first met him, she felt safe.

Pulling away from him, Kate said, "Do you think you could pull the mattress down so I can unpick it to wash the cover. We'll have to get more straw. Oh, and the two rugs."

"I've taken orders from the Captain since I was a boy and now I'm replacing them with orders from a wife. Oh! What am I doing?" His laugh was loud and contagious.

"I'll borrow a broom and bucket and come down here to clean in the next few days," Kate told him. "Perhaps I could put the fire on to air the place."

"Don't do anything till I've checked the chimney. It might be blocked," Freddie told her. "Come on, we'd better get back before they change the locks and we can't get in."

. . .

It was later in the evening when Kate was sitting in bed talking to Rachel that realisation at what she was doing hit her.

"Am I really doing the right thing, Rachel?" Kate asked. "I care for him well enough. What do you think?"

"I don't think anything about him…" Rachel didn't finish.

"What's wrong with him?"

"Nothing's wrong with him but I don't care for him romantically. I'm not like you, Kate, I don't think of men like that. I'm happy on my own. If you're not sure, you still have the option to go to New Zealand, to John."

"There's no point in going there if Clara's not there. What if I set off for New Zealand and she comes home? Ha! Home. I haven't got a home. I'm sure I'll be happy with Freddie. It won't be the same as Ted, that was once in a lifetime. It just won't be the same without you or Clara close by." Kate was on the verge of tears.

"Don't start that again. Life's what you make it. Only you can decide. I'll be here for the wedding and you've always got Mary and Amy here. Anyway, you'll be able to make friends." Rachel looked at her.

"Will you write to me often?" Kate asked. "I really will miss you."

"Yes, well, I'll miss you so let's both try to be happy," Rachel told her.

Freddie took a couple of the men to sort out the chimney and carry over plenty of wood. He wanted to move in but they didn't have a pot or plate, never mind any bedding. He was nothing but resourceful, going to the stables at Rathbone Hall for straw bales for the mattress, once the cover was dry. The cost would be taken from his wage.

Kate on the other hand didn't know how they could ever

manage, neither of them had any money to purchase even basic food so decided to stay where they were for now.

The mornings of the first week, Kate spent giving the place a good clean before returning to help Mary.

It was one of those afternoons when she was brought to tears.

"I want to give you this as a wedding gift," Mary told her, holding out an eiderdown. "It's been in my trunk for years. I can't bear to use it."

It had a smell of mothballs, scraps of material embroidered together on the front of a sheet. The inside was filled with lambswool which gave it warmth.

"Mary, it's beautiful. I couldn't possibly…"

"Take it, Kate. It's doing nothing sitting there. It needs airing but I want it to be used." Mary touched the material. "I made it for when I married but, well, he never returned and I couldn't use it."

Kate could see how much it meant to Mary, the memories it held and she was grateful. "What was his name?"

"Tommy Pincher. He was a stable lad at the hall," Mary told her, taking a chair to sit. "As soon as the Captain said he was joining the army, my Tommy went with him. A couple of the lads here were labourers at the hall and that's why they're here."

"I didn't know that," Kate told her. "My son, you know, Edward was lost. He was just a boy. I suppose they were all someone's boys."

"Aye, well, life has to go on no matter how the heart aches." Mary went to stir the soup, which was bubbling away on the stove for lunch. "The two lasses are Tommy's sisters. They would have ended up in the workhouse if the Captain hadn't taken them in. They're like daughters to me."

"My word, so he has got a heart. I didn't realise. I know the men think highly of him," Kate said, surprised.

"He's like a son to me, even though he's not much younger," Mary told her. "Now, let's not get maudlin."

It was later that evening when Kate was talking to Freddie about the Captain that she realised she had him all wrong. Apparently, he blamed himself for losing so many of his men but the orders had been flawed. The area they were heading for hadn't had any reconnaissance. They were lucky all was not lost. She asked him if he knew Captain Benson. He didn't, but told her they would be at Fort Frederick. Although peace had been declared, they wouldn't venture as far as Fort Albert without a troop of soldiers or the Boers, but many of them had returned to their farms. They would have to head toward the Drakensburg Mountains, crossing the Great Fish River which was dangerous.

Kate didn't know whether she was relieved or worried about where Clara was.

Rachel gave Kate £20 as a wedding gift to buy items for her home. It was a lot of money but Kate couldn't refuse it and it would also have to keep them until Freddie received a wage. She went to the market, buying the minimum, a kettle, large pan, frying pan along with cups, plates and cutlery. It was all second-hand and somewhat well used and battered but she didn't care.

Kate relented by writing another letter to Clara. She felt she would settle better if she reached out to her again, sooner rather than later. She decided not to send the original letter. Kate didn't want her to read it alone, so just told her where she was and that she was re-marrying. This didn't mean she would ever forget Ted or Edward and she stressed that Clara was still a daughter to her.

Freddie offered to take it to the post office as he had messages to complete in the village.

Kate sighed with relief when it was gone. All she could do now was wait. It shouldn't take so long to arrive in Port Elizabeth. She realised Clara wasn't her first and last thought each day… her heart wasn't aching so much for her. It was as Rachel said, she was a resourceful girl who had made her own decisions and was quite a capable young woman. She would always be her daughter, her little girl and she was what was left of the life before. Now she had a chance to make a new life with Freddie and was going to take it with both hands.

It was the week before the wedding when Kate decided she needed to speak to the Captain and thank him for his hospitality. She followed Archie into the rooms.

"You've got a visitor," Archie said gruffly before taking his leave.

"Ah, Mrs Williams, soon to be Mrs Stewart, congratulations," the Captain stated.

Kate wasn't sure if he was being sarcastic so replied with a thank you.

"So what do I owe this visitation?" he asked.

Now she knew he was being sarcastic. "Well," Kate said, "firstly I wanted to see how you were but also to thank you for your hospitality and kindness. I don't know where I would be now without your support."

"I'm sure a resourceful woman like yourself would have found something."

"I couldn't find anything in Middlesbrough and if it wasn't for Lady Evelyn Bellamy's family, I wouldn't be here now." Kate decided to be more open with him.

"Intriguing… how do you know the Bellamys? Please, Mrs Williams, take a seat." The Captain waved his arm.

Kate knew he would know some of her story so explained again how she came to be here and her connection with the Bellamys. The Captain didn't interrupt until Kate finished by telling him about Clara and Captain Benson's wife, when he laughed.

"I've met Mrs Benson. Nice to look at but not much in here…" The Captain tapped his head. "Miss Clara will need to be able to ignore the onslaught of chatter."

"I doubt it. She's very headstrong and has a temper on her," Kate responded, laughing with him.

"Oh, poor Captain Benson. He'll be spending much of his time in the Officers' Club." He laughed again. Then added, "I've enjoyed our talks. It's a shame you won't be here much longer."

"I won't be far away, so I could always call in. I was going to ask you how you felt about me coming over to help Mary when she's busy?"

It was agreed she would come over in the mornings to help on washday and aid Amy as well as Mary. Just before she took her leave, Kate decided to ask the question she had really come for.

"We would both love it if you would do us the honour of attending our wedding. It will be a very small affair."

"No, it's impossible. I can see where Miss Clara gets her character from. What I am prepared to do is arrange a wedding breakfast here. I'll speak to Mary," the Captain told her.

"That's more than kind of you. Freddie will love to be amongst his friends. It's just…" Kate didn't get to say anymore.

"Let's not fall out, Mrs Williams. I hope we can remain friends?" he asked.

"Yes, of course. Perhaps in the summer, when you're feeling better, you could visit me." Kate stood to leave.

"We'll see. Now, I'm sure you have plenty to organise." The Captain turned from her.

CHAPTER 30

KATE AND RACHEL, LONDON 1904

Suddenly it was the night before her wedding at the end of January. Kate was nervous about tomorrow's event. They had no money to buy a ring so she had removed the wedding ring Ted had given her for only the second time since they married. Freddie promised he would buy her a new one as soon as finances allowed.

She didn't mind, really she didn't as it meant Ted was still with her. He would always have a place in her heart. As she handed the ring to Freddie, he took her in his arms.

"I wanted to give you a gift before the wedding but didn't know what would be suitable," he told her.

"I don't need a gift, Freddie. Let's just be happy, that's enough," Kate told him.

"Well, I did think of something and I hope you are not cross with me, or call off the wedding. I wrote to Clara to tell her I wasn't trying to replace her father, but hoped we could be friends. Also that she would always have a home with us. I put my letter in with yours." He waited expectantly for a reply.

"I didn't want to cry the night before my wedding but that

is so thoughtful, so kind. I don't know what else to say," Kate sobbed.

"Don't say anything. I'll see you tomorrow." Freddie kissed her gently before they went their separate ways.

THE WEDDING itself was a quiet affair with just those from the house in attendance. Kate was pleased once more to be wearing the coat with the fur trim around the collar and cuffs. Freddie was in his uniform. He had polished his shoes until he could see his face in them. The rest of the men also looked very smart. The only people left in the house were the Captain and Archie.

Saying her wedding vows, Kate realised she was content with her life which was now set with Freddie Stewart. He was a kind man with unruly blond hair, which had been cut short for today. He looked proud to wear his army uniform and his eyes sparkled when she smiled nervously at him.

Walking down the aisle, arm in arm, Mr and Mrs Stewart, Kate and Freddie acknowledged the small congregation from the house. Once outside the church, the men patted Freddie heartily on his back while Kate hugged Rachel, Mary and the two girls.

The wedding breakfast was a cold buffet but the greatest surprise was Captain Gibson Park, immaculate in his officer's uniform, who made an entrance into the room, holding on to Archie. Those who could stand did as they saluted. Kate could see how much he meant to the men as a cheer went up. He raised a glass to the newlyweds. Each of the men listened to his every word in their own way, including Freddie, who took Kate's hand in thanks.

When it was time to leave for the small cottage, Kate clung to Rachel to say goodbye. She was leaving for Durham early the following morning. Kate was afraid she would never see her again.

"Go on, get yourself away with your husband." Rachel pulled away from her.

"Please make sure you write," Kate sobbed.

"Don't spoil your day. I'll write as soon as I can. Just be happy, Kate." Rachel hugged her again.

KATE LINKED Freddie's arm as they walked past Rathbone Hall to the cottage where their new life was to begin. Freddie climbed up the ladder to the bedroom where he began removing his uniform as he had to go to work. Kate followed him up and saw for the first time the scar on his back where a spear had struck his shoulder. She gently reached out to touch it. He turned, taking her into his arms. She found she wanted him as much as he wanted her and they clung to each other.

As they lay together in the marital bed, Kate knew her life was set with this man, a brave man who she realised she loved. He groaned and she looked at him.

"I've got to go to work, Mrs Stewart. Don't want to get sacked for being late." He kissed her gently.

"Well, best get on your way, Mr Stewart. Don't let me stop you."

"You know you'll always stop me." Freddie got up. "I've got to go but be sure to be waiting for me when I get back." He laughed.

"Yes sir." Kate saluted, pulling the eiderdown up to her chin.

LIFE FOR KATE got into another routine. Once Freddie left for work, she went up to the house to help Mary for the morning, having her lunch there. She was comfortable in the company of the men and they seemed to accept her. She would bring bread, butter, cheese or a warm meal for later in the day and she was more than grateful to Mary for this.

At the cottage, she collected water from the pipe by the cottages daily. Spring arrived with the melting snow, snowdrops and daffodils along the hedgerows giving colour. Kate wanted to do something in the small garden but the ground was still hard. She pulled and tugged at weeds which she placed in a pile to dry before burning. The ash from the fire she used to make a path to the gate.

In the evening, Kate and Freddie would sit on the kitchen chairs, chatting happily about their day. Both seemed content with the life they were making.

Rachel had written, telling Kate she was busy training a new batch of nurses. She was happy and settled. Spring turned into longer summer days when Freddie would occasionally go out in the evening with his new dog, Finn, who followed him everywhere. It was as if Kate didn't exist unless she was offering food. It was fortunate Finn couldn't get up the ladder, she thought, otherwise she would be pushed out of the bed.

She couldn't believe the year was heading toward autumn and still no contact from Clara. Her heart didn't ache anymore and although she mentioned her in her prayers every night, Kate had learnt to live without her.

She sat in the light of the fire, repairing her husband's socks. She should really light one of the lamps to stop straining her eyes but the need to be careful with money had never left her, though Freddie's wage was more than enough to keep them comfortably. Kate tried to save a little each week as she worried they would be turned out for whatever reason and be in a worse state than before with no home or job. Freddie always laughed at her. He would find something, he told her and he had no intention of losing his job. With all the walking he did, he was tanned and slimmer, his back straight. He would often supplement their food with rabbits or pigeons though he would have to skin them for her.

She was happy even though the place was small. Her friends were at the house, her neighbours pleasant. She regularly took the two girls to the village on market day. Kate could see her and Freddie growing old together in the grounds of Rathbone Hall, God willing.

She didn't look up when she heard the latch on the cottage door open. "Hello, love. You're home early."

There was no immediate reply. She turned her head toward the dimming light as someone came in through the door. Kate turned her head, the darning falling to the floor as her hand went to her throat. She cried out.

"Hello, mam," Clara said.

EPILOGUE

LOTTE AGED 20, WELLINGTON NEW ZEALAND 2013

Lotte spent the rest of her holiday researching the family link to the Linthorpe Pottery. She clicked on the keys of her laptop as ideas flowed. Some nights she spent hours writing and re-writing her story, much to the chagrin of younger sister Brogan who complained she couldn't sleep.

The printer churned out page after page to be edited but Lotte had so many ideas she didn't want to stop until her novel was finished.

She was so excited at what had been gleaned by reading the letters to her great, great grandfather John from his sister Kate. They felt so close. It made her sad she had never met them but the letters gave her a good insight into their lives.

Taking what she considered a welcome break, Lotte went out into the garden where her gran was pottering, a pair of secateurs in her hands.

"Hello, lovely. I hear you've been busy, too busy to have a coffee with your old gran."

"I've got time now. My novel is almost finished but I could do with a fresh pair of eyes to read it. Are you up for it, Gran?" Lotte asked.

"As long as it's not one of those bodice rippers full of sex and heaving bosoms," she laughed. "You know I like a good mystery."

"No, of course not, but you might like it as it's sort of family. I have used some poetic license to fill in what I don't know."

LOTTE STOOD by the side of the stage, in her cap and gown, waiting for her name to be called. Gran and her parents were sitting in the auditorium, proud she had passed her course with flying colours. The novel had been well received by her tutors and later this week she was speaking to a publisher. She had even been offered a job at the Te Papa Museum as a researcher, logging all the new ceramics they had been given, a post she accepted immediately.

"Charlotte Taylor, Certificate in Journalism and Creative Writing," the Chancellor called.

Lotte stepped forward to receive her certificate to the loud applause of the audience.

ALSO BY BERYL ROBINSON

A Life of Consequence

Married to a brutal man more than twice her age, Hannah is young, pregnant and despairing. One day she can take no more and one single action forces her to flee. Accepting help from a stranger, she escapes to a new life where she finds happiness at last.

Grant My Last Request

For Hannah Phelan, life is hard in Australia. Each time she thinks she has turned a corner, and managed to hold her family together, something stops her. Now a widow with two small children, it seems someone knows about her life before, in England, a secret she has to keep at all costs.

Available on Amazon for Kindle and in paperback.

Printed in Great Britain
by Amazon